The Couples Therapy Toolbox

The Couples Therapy Toolbox

75+ Exercises to Improve and
Strengthen Your Relationship

Danielle Duchatellier Boucree, MSW, LCSW-C, MBA

ROCKRIDGE
PRESS

To my parents, whose breathtaking love I had the honor of experiencing for 56 years. I learned how to love by watching you. I love you.

Contents

Introduction

Welcome to the next phase of your relationship journey. This is an incredible step that you've decided to take together, and I'm so excited to be a part of it. This workbook is designed to engage you in a vast array of exercises that will take your connection to a new level.

In my clinical work as a licensed social worker and psychotherapist specializing in couples, I've encountered many people ready for change. I've helped to guide them, through consistent hard work, to achieve their goals. For instance, I have worked with couples getting ready to make a lifelong commitment, newlyweds looking to start their lives together, couples looking to repair damage done to their relationship, and partners with decades of marriage looking for refinements. Regardless of the relationship stage in which you find yourself, there's always work that can be done to be your best together. Personally, I wish I'd had access to the tools presented in *The Couples Therapy Toolbox* when I started considering marriage. It would have helped me avoid some difficult times during transitions like new jobs, new homes, and the introduction of children.

Keep in mind that although this workbook is a great way to optimize your relationship, it is not meant to stand alone therapeutically. If you or your partner show signs of any mental health difficulties like anxiety or depression, it is best that you seek professional help, therapy, medical treatment, or medication. Group therapy is also an efficient resource for mental health support, providing access to both clinical professionals and a community.

I am eager to guide you as you continue learning, connecting, and growing in your relationship. Thank you for trusting me to take this ride with you. If you put the work in, you'll come out of this experience as a better team.

-Danielle

How to Use This Book

The Couples Therapy Toolbox offers information and activities for connection and improvement on the aspects of your relationship that need support. Each chapter delves into a different topic, so they can be used either independently or together. The idea is that you can choose what you'd like to work on based on the aspects of your relationship that need support. If an activity doesn't apply to your situation now, skip it. Before you start, talk about what prompted you to reach for this workbook, so you can determine your shared goals and ideal outcomes.

Part I of *The Couples Therapy Toolbox* focuses on defining healthy relationship dynamics and introduces you to a range of therapeutic concepts. The goal is to come to a shared understanding of what behaviors tend to support or hinder healthy growth in a relationship. This part defines the terms and concepts to prepare you both to take on the therapeutically-inspired exercises found in part II.

Part II contains seventy-seven exercises to do together to build on the foundation set up in the first two chapters of the book. Each one features space for both partners to respond, either through open writing or directed Q&A. Use part II of this workbook in any order based on your immediate needs, and return to the exercises whenever you feel the need to work further on specific skills. Check in with each other after each exercise to make sure you are both ready to move on from that topic. If you feel emotionally worn out, take a break and agree on a time to continue. It is not necessary to complete exercises in any specific period of time. Pace yourselves so that you both enjoy the process of refining your relationship.

PART I

THE FUNDAMENTALS OF A HEALTHY RELATIONSHIP

Before diving into the interactive exercises provided in this workbook, it is important for both of you to understand what makes a relationship healthy. This part of the book will describe and define what constitutes a healthy relationship and set out some of the characteristics of an unhealthy relationship. You will also set relationship goals together, learn that there are specific ways to improve your relationship, and understand how to create a safe space where you can feel vulnerable and heard when participating in the exercises.

CHAPTER 1

Healthy Relationships 101

The very act of working toward a healthy relationship can be an incredibly rewarding experience. It is not necessarily a linear process: At times, you may feel like you are progressing beautifully; other times you may feel like you are working hard but going nowhere. Setting specific goals, with both partners aligned, helps make the growth process a smoother one. Goals allow you to measure your progress, hold yourselves accountable, and determine what areas need additional attention. But before you set goals for a healthy relationship, you have to be able to define what one is. This chapter lays out the parameters of a healthy relationship. It also identifies the signs of an unhealthy relationship, as well as how to avoid common pitfalls.

What Is a Healthy Relationship?

What makes a relationship healthy is wholly dependent on the two people trying to connect. The number of variables that go into relationship health are as varied as the people in the relationships. Influences may include the stories each partner heard growing up, what they experienced day to day, and their dating history, just to name a few. It's really quite amazing when two people come together and connect. After that initial connection, it takes effort to create and sustain a healthy relationship, and there are some foundational behaviors, like trust, that tend to be beneficial for most couples.

Think of the elements of healthy relationships like a three-tiered cake. The bottom layer is the largest, and its strength is required for the cake to stand tall. In most relationships, the bottom layer includes trust, communication, and intimacy. The middle layer of the cake is smaller but still critical. It represents the foundation upon which the top layer must sit. Mutual respect and healthy boundaries make up the middle layer. Finally, the top tier is the quality most people admire: equal partnership. To create this sculptural confection, each partner must be cognizant of the ingredients in all three layers and avoid additives like codependency and manipulation, which can topple the whole thing.

The Foundations of a Healthy Relationship

From the outside, some people may admire a couple that has been together since high school. Others may look at a couple who met later in life after each had the opportunity to develop as a separate individual and see that relationship as healthy. Who's right? The truth is that neither one is necessarily more successful than the other. There is no one factor, like duration, that makes a relationship healthy. But generally, relationships cannot be healthy if they do not have trust, communication, respect, boundaries, partnership, healthy conflict, and shared intimacy. Are you expected to be perfect at all of the aspects that make up a healthy relationship? Absolutely not. But it is a realistic expectation for both partners to work to be better than they were yesterday. It is progress, not perfection, that leads to relationship success. Consider how these foundational elements of most healthy relationships come into play and why they are beneficial.

Trust

Trust is more than a measure of the existence or absence of deceit. It represents a feeling of safety with one's physical and emotional self at the hands of another. Over the course of a relationship, when both parties can be vulnerable with one another, trust grows. On the flip side, it can be broken as quickly as it takes to pop a balloon. The beauty of trust within any relationship is that it creates a space for honesty, open communication, vulnerability, and respect. With trust present, you can believe your partner has your best interest at heart and won't try to hurt you.

Open Communication

Open and honest communication occurs when each partner is comfortable being transparent without fear of negative consequences hurtful to the relationship. You are both able to express yourselves without fear of judgment and do so freely. Honest communication is vital to a healthy relationship because partners need the forum to be able to share their emotions and their thoughts and receive validation and empathy, two important elements in communication. Open communication enhances trust and strengthens the foundations of the relationship.

Mutual Respect

Mutual respect refers to recognizing and appreciating that your partner has a history outside of your relationship and that they have thoughts, opinions, and qualities that have inherent value. The presence of mutual respect allows each partner to feel like their thoughts and feelings matter, like *they* matter. More concrete aspects of mutual respect include consent, agreeing on a pace to move the relationship forward, and accountability for words and actions. This respect results in an environment of safety within the relationship: safety to express yourself, safety to be genuine, and safety to be honest.

Healthy Boundaries

Boundaries are the parameters that need to be determined to define your personal limits within a relationship—what you are willing to take or give before feeling uncomfortable. At first, boundary-setting can feel selfish. This kind of change can feel awkward because you may be taking an assertive stance that you have never taken before, and you may be uncertain of the outcome. But setting boundaries is actually a gift to the relationship. It helps promote safety and comfort, leading to emotional wellness and closeness and allowing genuine growth.

Equal Partnership

Equal partnership in a relationship means that neither partner has considerably more of their desires or needs met than the other. Both partners are committed to hearing one another and respecting each other's voice. There is alignment in the goals of the relationship, and both parties work equally to meet those goals. This equality makes the relationship healthy because it removes the possibility that either partner feels taken for granted or unappreciated. What is so special about an equal partnership is that it feels supportive and safe and ultimately leads to less conflict and resentment.

Healthy Conflict

When individuals unite, conflict happens. Healthy relationships maintain boundaries even in conflict. For example, if you're triggered by cursing during conflict, you can set a "no cursing" boundary. Go ahead and advocate for what you believe to be true, but stay away from verbally attacking your partner. And if your partner makes the effort to be vulnerable, try to listen and validate their emotions and thoughts. Fight the urge to keep belaboring your points in a disagreement. Ultimately, everyone wants to be heard. Taking time to listen as well as to speak will ensure equity and lead to quicker resolution.

Shared Intimacy

Many assume intimacy refers only to the sexual aspects of a relationship. But shared intimacy is much broader. It includes a mutual closeness based on emotional connection. Intimacy can show up as vulnerability, honesty, making your partner your priority, or having the comfort to rely on your partner unconditionally. Be aware that it's not always something that appears early in your relationship but builds over time. Shared intimacy is important to a healthy relationship and to both of you individually, in part because it meets your basic physiological needs, whether through a simple touch or a sexual connection.

Common Signs of an Unhealthy Relationship

In a healthy relationship, individuals come together to enhance each other's lived experiences and bring out positive traits in one another. No relationship is perfect, but feelings of strain and disconnection may be signs that you're in an unhealthy situation. Recognizing the signs of a relationship breaking down will allow you to begin to address the areas in need of repair. Signs of an unhealthy relationship include, but are not limited to:

- Possessiveness
- Manipulation
- Abuse
- Codependency

Whether the difficulty in your relationship is centered around possessiveness, manipulation, abuse, or codependency, transparency within the relationship will help as you are striving to improve it. So, start talking and lead with emotions and openness.

Possessiveness

Possessiveness is about an intention of control over your partner. What can start out as seemingly thoughtful gestures, like calling numerous times daily, can shift to a more negative feeling of possessiveness when the intention becomes about control. Possessiveness can manifest as physical, like if your partner always needs to know where you are, or if they do not respect your personal boundaries. It might also be emotional, like if your partner expects you to respond to their needs immediately, at all times. Lastly, it could manifest socially, in attempts to control your relationships with others. Possessiveness breaks down the foundations of a relationship, namely trust and mutual respect.

Manipulation

Manipulative behaviors are actions used by one partner to control the other's thoughts and feelings, often by playing on their insecurities or moving the goalpost for a previously-set expectation. The signs can be subtle or direct. They can come in the form of love bombing, a flooding of affection; this level of affection from your partner crosses the line to manipulation when something is expected in return. Or, manipulation may take the form of gaslighting, where your partner makes you question what you know to be true. No matter how you slice it, manipulation breaks down your connection and chips away at the self-confidence of the partner being manipulated.

Abuse

Abuse in relationships can be physical, emotional, psychological, sexual, or financial. Physical abuse, for example, is the use of physical force causing harm. It includes such behavior as hitting, choking, or restraining. Emotional abuse affects feelings. It is any attempt to control using such tactics as criticism, humiliation, and manipulation. Even though it leaves no physical scars, it can be equally harmful to your relationship. Financial abuse involves taking control of your partner's ability to make, spend, or save money. All abuse is based on the abuser's need for power. It has a negative impact on relationships because of the imbalance of power and broken trust it creates.

Codependency

A codependent relationship is a dysfunctional relationship that will likely become destructive in nature. Essentially, one partner believes they need the other partner, and the other partner's self-worth is defined by the sacrifices they make for their partner. Both partners feed off their interdependent needs and the cycle is difficult to break. Partners in a codependent relationship find it generally unrewarding. It doesn't allow a genuine equal partnership to develop and lacks transparency, respect, and often, intimacy.

Note: These signs of an unhealthy relationship are a representative list not meant to be exhaustive. If you find yourself in an abusive relationship and need help, the National Domestic Violence Hotline (800) 799-7233 is available 24/7.

Self-Assessment: What Are Your Relationship Goals?

To avoid operating aimlessly, it's important to identify areas of potential growth and to set relationship goals on which both of you can agree and focus. Take fifteen to twenty minutes doing this assessment to establish yours. After setting goals, both partners will feel a shift in the right direction in your relationship.

1. If safe to do so, talk through recent conflicts or difficult moments in your relationship. What were the situations? What made it difficult for each of you? What might have made it easier? Be careful to talk about the occurrences without being critical of one another. You want to make each other feel heard, validated, and understood. If either of you feels defensive, despite efforts to stay open to feedback, it could mean the conversation has shifted toward criticism.

2. To guide you, imagine this example. You and your partner recently argued about how neither of you tends to apologize, instead making excuses during conflict. In this case, your goal as a couple may be a dual one: to lessen defensiveness and improve accountability.

3. Like any other goals, those you identify for your relationship will require commitment. It's time to put your commitment on paper to keep you both answerable to working on your goals. But first, identify them. In the following chart, identify three relationship goals, then list specific challenges you are experiencing in your relationship that might stand in the way of reaching those goals.

GOALS	CURRENT CHALLENGES
Goal 1:	
Goal 2:	
Goal 3:	

This frank, robust discussion is meant to allow you to reflect on the current state of your partnership, align on ways to improve what is already strong, and work on what may need some tweaking. When you have completed the this book, come back to these goals and make note of your progress and where work is still required. With stated common goals, you have every reason to hope for an even better tomorrow.

Relationships Take Time to Nurture

Working to make your relationship healthier requires hard work and a positive mindset that your efforts will lead to a desired outcome. Reading this book together and completing chapter 1 shows how willing you are to seek positive change in your relationship.

Keep in mind that it takes time, patience, and consistent effort. Give yourselves grace for the well-meaning mistakes you may make along the way. This is a journey you are taking together to make your shared lives as fulfilling as possible for both of you. Pledge to each other to be your best selves and make necessary sacrifices because you are hopeful that you can be better to each other and for each other. Life will happen. Other responsibilities, social or professional, will come up. These may pull your attention in different directions or make demands on your time and energy. Make time to focus on strengthening your bond with one another. Be patient with yourselves and with each other, knowing that the fact that you are making the effort is a sign of commitment. Honor your commitment and honor each other.

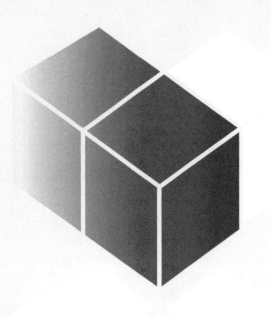

CHAPTER 2

Working Together toward a Healthy Relationship

Optimize your love with a positive outlook. To live in a healthy relationship together, it is important to realize that positivity and belief in one another play a crucial part in your ability to work toward common goals. This chapter will help you set guidelines so you can navigate this workbook most effectively. It will review strategies to create your own path to a healthier relationship. You'll notice the importance of showing each other patience and assuming good intent. Most of all, the chapter will offer you tips on how to show up in your relationship every day, whether you're working through the exercises in this workbook or taking a break.

There Are Many Ways to Improve Your Relationship

People typically set clear expectations and ground rules that let others know how to treat them. The same applies to your relationship. As a unit, you need to come together and figure out the guidelines that will strengthen your unique partnership. As you entered the relationship, you may have had ideas about how your partner would be and the role they would play in your life. Those preferences were based on your individual needs, your lifestyle, and how you prefer to receive love, among other things. For each person, those ideas are different. So, it's important to come together as a team and figure out which ones suit you both.

As you decide on these guidelines, give yourselves grace and understanding. You will make progress through intention and effort, but the rate at which you see improvement is not predetermined. Do not get discouraged. Instead, enjoy the journey. By working together on the exercises in this book, you'll gain a deeper understanding of each other and your ultimate connection.

Aim for Progress over Perfection

As you are assessing your relationship, recognizing transitions over time and reorienting toward the future are both important. Look at where you are *today* in setting goals. Trying to get back to where you used to be is only setting yourselves up for failure. You may not experience your relationship like it used to be, but that's okay. The relationship that lies ahead will likely be better with improved understanding and a more concrete connection. It is more important that you recognize progress in yourselves than that you achieve any level of perfection.

On the other hand, celebrating progress leads to connection with each other. Let doing your best be good enough; focus on the small successes toward your goals and keep moving forward so you both can thrive. Remember, your relationship is one of a kind. Know that your love story started with a connection that was organically imperfect and all the more beautiful for it.

SIMPLE TIPS TO TRY EVERY DAY

To build a healthy relationship, some people look to self-help books, talk to friends, or participate in therapy. These are all outstanding options and can help you notice and address unhealthy habits in your relationship. But they are not the only options. There are a myriad of ways to improve your relationship without taking a chunk of time, money, or energy. You can tap into these to supplement your work with this book:

- Become a consistent, active listener: Be fully present in conversations, and try to go beyond the words your partner is saying to the message behind them. Then signal through verbal and physical cues that you are paying attention.

- Take ten minutes to connect in the morning before you start your day: Ask your partner how they feel about the day ahead, validate feelings, and show support for each other.

- Take another ten minutes to intentionally listen to your partner after the day is done: Ask open-ended follow-up questions that begin with prompts like "Tell me about" or "Help me understand" to foster a deeper connection and understanding.

- Listen to and respect boundaries set by your partner.

- Schedule at least one hour of quality time together without interruption per week: Unplug and focus on each other. If you engage in an activity together, try to choose one that makes you feel more connected with each other.

- Express gratitude *for* each other and *to* each other every day.

At the end of each week, sit down and have a brief discussion on how you're doing. This can be an incentive to be realistic about which of the above options you can both commit to.

Creating Space to Work Together

The Couples Therapy Toolbox is broken down into a series of exercises by topic. Some of the activities may be challenging or provoke intense feelings. They require a willingness to dive deeply into your emotions and to do so with vulnerability and transparency. You may feel uncomfortable at times, but you'll need to work together to create a safe space to explore those complicated thoughts and emotions. A safe space means that you can share your thoughts and concerns without fear of escalation into conflict or retaliation.

These tools, which will help you approach the exercises more comfortably, include, but are not limited to, being intentionally thankful to your partner for their contribution, using positive body language and touch, conducting mindfulness exercises together regularly, and creating a safe space to work together.

Gratitude Mindset: A gratitude mindset, in this case, means being intentionally thankful for your partner's commitment to the activities in this workbook. It can be tough to hear how your words and actions may be negatively affecting your partner. It can be difficult to explore how experiences outside of your relationship may have influenced them in painful ways. When you hear something that's hard for you to process, it can help to remember that your partner is being open, honest, and vulnerable, and that they are doing the work of sharing something challenging in order to work toward your joint relationship goals. Let your partner know how much you appreciate their candor and transparency.

Positive Body Language and Touch: At times, non-verbal communication is as important as verbal communication. Regardless of the words you use, your non-verbal cues affect your message. It can be confusing if those cues do not match up with your words, but, on the other hand, when they do match, the cues can enhance your message. When trying to connect with your partner, it can help to avoid turning your back, rolling your eyes, or sitting at a distance. These can make your partner feel unheard or judged, even if that is not your goal. Instead, turn toward your partner, make loving eye contact, and be aware of your facial expressions. When listening, nod to validate what they are saying to you. Touch their hands or legs as a sign of support.

Conduct Mindfulness Exercises Together: Participating in a mindful meditation together can include deep or measured breathing, trying to clear or calm your mind, and noticing any thoughts that come up and letting them go without judgment. If you are new to this practice, you can find free guided meditations for beginners on phone apps or online videos. The more you practice mindfulness, the easier it may be to approach new or emotionally charged situations with calm and avoid a reactionary response. When applied to the exercises in part II of this book, mindfulness can help you slow down and focus on them and on one another.

Creating Space to Work Together: Choose the space where you will work through the exercises in this workbook carefully. It should be a quiet space where you can have full privacy to ensure that both of you are comfortable expressing yourselves clearly, honestly, and vulnerably. You should both be physically comfortable in your attire and the place you sit. Make sure you have enough room to sit side by side to share the contents of the workbook and to conduct the exercises together. The day of the week or time of day is less important than your consistency. I recommend setting aside two days per week, for one to two hours per sitting, to work through the exercises you choose. Do what is best for both of you, and commit.

It's Never Too Late to Mend Your Relationship

Congratulations! You're here and ready to put some effort into your relationship. Whether you've picked up this workbook to strengthen your foundation, to address a feeling of disconnect, or because your trust and commitment have taken a hit and you are searching for tools to repair them, you're in the right place. Whatever the situation, whether it has just occurred or has been decades in the making, this workbook can help you be intentional in your attempts to grow closer together; now is the time.

As you complete the exercises in this book, check in regularly to assess how you both feel in your relationship. Measure your growth and how much closer you are to your relationship goals. It's okay to not be okay, to feel overwhelmed by the process, or to feel like it's going slower than you had hoped. But there is always time to improve your relationship.

And, it's also okay to ask for help from a professional if you feel like you've not gotten close enough to mending the parts of your relationship that feel broken. There is strength of purpose and courage in asking for help to build your relationship. That assistance can come from a therapist, a spiritual leader, a community you participate in, or another source, depending on your needs, access, and values (see Resources, page 127). Keep in mind that asking for help is a stride toward the future rather than an indictment on where you are at this point or how you got here. Consider seeking outside assistance to supplement this book at any point and for any reason, including the following:

- If you're struggling to communicate effectively

- If one or both of you have had an affair

- If conflicts tend to keep building instead of ending in resolution

PART II

TOOLS TO HELP YOU IMPROVE AND STRENGTHEN YOUR RELATIONSHIP

Now that you have reviewed the elements of a healthy and unhealthy relationship and explored ways to approach this workbook emotionally and mentally, it's time to get started working through some activities. The chapters that follow are separated by the elements of a healthy relationship: building trust, communicating effectively, establishing respect, creating healthy boundaries, having healthy conflict, fostering an equal partnership, and nurturing intimacy. You can follow them sequentially or you can review all seven topics and decide which ones are priorities for your relationship based on your predetermined goals. There is no correct way to complete this workbook. Do what you and your partner feel is best and know that you can revisit any chapter anytime.

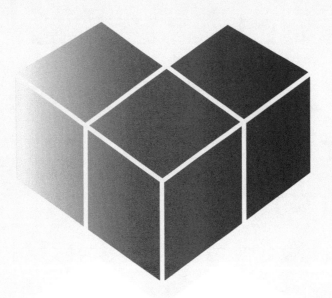

CHAPTER 3

Build Trust

Trust between partners is important to a relationship because it allows both people to feel safe in sharing the details of their lives and their inner selves. In this chapter, you will be challenged to assess and enhance your trust in each other by discussing your vulnerabilities and your needs. You will be asked to look at your emotional triggers and to be transparent about them. You will be tasked with noticing and addressing signs that trust may be missing. And you will find specific tools to build and repair trust in your relationship. With a little hope and a lot of honesty, you can deepen your connection, become a stronger team in the present, and clarify your shared vision of the future.

Trust Assessment

Take a minute to measure the level of trust in your relationship today. The best way to know where you are going is to know where you currently stand.

Each partner should read the following questions and use a different color ink to circle their responses using this scale: 0 = Not at all, 1 = Rarely, 2 = Sometimes, 3 = Frequently, 4 = Most Often, 5 = Always.

When both partners have completed the quiz, use the key at the bottom of the page for scoring. If large discrepancies are identified in your answers, discuss those questions together for greater understanding.

I feel comfortable telling my partner anything.	0 1 2 3 4 5
I know my partner will offer me support when I need it.	0 1 2 3 4 5
I am certain my partner will not embarrass me in front of others.	0 1 2 3 4 5
I do not need to ask my partner about their whereabouts.	0 1 2 3 4 5
I am comfortable having my partner make decisions that will affect me personally.	0 1 2 3 4 5
My partner's behavior is consistent and predictable.	0 1 2 3 4 5
I know my partner feels comfortable sharing their vulnerable thoughts with me.	0 1 2 3 4 5

I am sure my partner will not cheat on me.	0	1	2	3	4	5
My partner keeps promises.	0	1	2	3	4	5
I am confident my partner tells me the truth even when the explanation sounds suspicious.	0	1	2	3	4	5

SCORING

Add up your points and see where you stand.

0–15 points: Need to Develop Trust. You and your partner are having trouble feeling trust in your relationship. Since trust is a critical element of relationship success, make all exercises in this chapter a priority.

16–35 points: Trust Could Use Some Focus. The trust between you and your partner is inconsistent. Consider making this chapter one of your top priorities as you work through this workbook.

36–50 points: Trust is a Foundation of your Relationship. You and your partner have developed and nurtured trust in your relationship. Though strong, trust needs consistency. Although this chapter might not be your top priority, make sure you come back to it because of its importance in maintaining a healthy relationship.

Let's Talk Trust Quotes

The concept of trust means different things to different people, even within the same relationship. One way to develop your own definition of what trust means to you is to think about the words others have said about trust and decide whether or not they resonate with you.

Separately, do some research to find quotes on the concept of trust that resonate with you. Next, decide on your five favorite quotes together and add them to the Quote Bank below. Together, read the collected quotes out loud and talk about what they mean to you. Then create a joint definition of what trust means to your relationship.

QUOTE BANK

1. ....

....

2. ....

....

3. ....

....

4. ....

....

5. ....

....

Our definition of trust is: ....

....

Trust Your Partner to Plan

Sometimes in a relationship, either partner might feel the need to control situations to avoid feeling anxious. There is usually an underlying reason. To determine the reasons behind the anxiety, take some deep breaths and document any thoughts that might be contributing to the feelings of anxiety. Then take those negative thoughts and consider the possible alternate positive thoughts. In this exercise, each of you will plan a date from beginning to end with no input from your partner. The purpose of this activity is to assess and increase your level of trust; relinquishing control is a sign of a strong level of trust in your partner.

1. Partner A will plan a date. Partner B can offer input on the day and time but nothing else. Go on the date together without giving any feedback or commentary on what you are enjoying or what you would have done differently.

2. Immediately after the date, Partner B should journal using the boxes below. Document how it felt for you, your positive and negative thoughts, and some of your reflections. End your journal entry with a statement of gratitude.

3. Repeat with Partner B taking the lead and Partner A journaling afterward.

PARTNER A   **PARTNER B**

When my partner planned the date I felt . . .

My thoughts were . . .

I was grateful for . . .

When both dates have been completed, talk about your thoughts and gratitude statements, and explore how giving up control affected your trust for your partner and how that felt.

Being Vulnerable Together

The risk behind being vulnerable is trusting that your partner will not judge, dismiss, or reject you as a result. But the rewards of improved connection and a healthier relationship are worth it. This exercise will help you and your partner exhibit some of your vulnerabilities to one another and practice hearing and feeling heard.

Use the table to list your fears and insecurities. Internal fears are tied to your self-worth. External fears are caused by an outside source, and relationship fears are ones that directly affect your relationship. You also have room for fears that cannot be categorized in this way. List as many as come to your mind in five minutes.

PARTNER A   **PARTNER B**

Internal

External

Relationship

Other

1. Read your list to your partner. Take turns.

2. Partner B should identify the top three fears on Partner A's list that they want more information on or feel they do not understand. Circle or highlight them.

3. Partner A should try to talk about the fears Partner B identified, while Partner B practices active listening by rephrasing back what they hear. Ask questions for clarification or understanding only.

4. Swap roles.

What Are Your Caution Triggers?

At times in your relationship, your instincts might identify a "red flag" or reason for caution. Don't ignore these instincts even though they might make you feel helpless, panicked, or unsafe. Instead, recognize them as possible triggers from past experiences. Lean into the discomfort that accompanies triggers, and talk about it together. In this exercise, you will assess the experiences from your past relationships that might contribute to this feeling of discomfort in your current relationship. Then you will share with your partner to strengthen trust between the two of you.

1. Reflect on past relationships and identify times when your trust was tested or broken. Include romantic, familial, and friend relationships.

2. How do these experiences trigger you in your relationship today? (For example, you might bring up that your previous partner had a codependent relationship with their mother; this triggers you when your current partner's mother wants to be a decision maker in your relationship.)

3. What do you need from your partner when you are feeling triggered? (For example, you might need your current partner to set boundaries with their mother.)

4. Complete the phrases below to identify triggers that you see as most impactful in your current relationship. Each partner should identify two examples.

PARTNER A

My trust was broken when: ....

....

....

I am triggered by: ....

....

I need: ....

....

My trust was broken when: ....

....

I am triggered by: ....

....

I need: ....

....

PARTNER B

My trust was broken when: ....

....

I am triggered by: ....

....

I need: ....

....

My trust was broken when: ....

....

I am triggered by: ....

....

I need: ....

....

What Are You Afraid Of? Name It!

Your experiences growing up may contribute to fears you have brought into your relationship. Those fears can unintentionally get in the way of you giving and receiving trust. By attempting to identify and face these fears together, you open a clearer path to trust in your relationship.

1. Think through your relationships with family, friends, and partners, and ways that trust may have been difficult in those relationships. Consider both physical and emotional trust.

2. In the following thought bubbles, write brief descriptions of your trust-related fears (four bubbles for each partner). Then explain each one to your partner, and allow your partner the opportunity to validate your fear by showing support through recognizing your feelings, asking questions to show interest, or just showing that they care. (For example, expression of trust-related fear: "I am afraid that if I ask you too many questions, you will get mad and leave me." Response: "It sounds like you're afraid I will leave you.")

3. When finished, each of you should choose your most potent fear and talk through how you feel about it now.

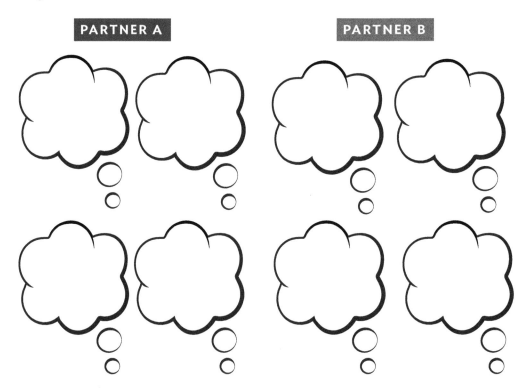

PARTNER A   PARTNER B

What Builds Trust?

Generally, trust is built on consistency of actions and words over time. It is important to reflect upon any situations in your relationship that helped build trust between you and your partner so that you can seek out ways to build on those moments moving forward.

In the following table, compile a list of experiences and expressions that have built trust in your relationship (e.g., talking each night before going to sleep or telling each other how attracted you are to one another). Recall specific instances and write them down. Discuss how you can both recreate similar opportunities to build trust in the future.

EXPERIENCES THAT HAVE BUILT TRUST	EXPRESSIONS THAT HAVE BUILT TRUST

Look Me in the Eye

One way to build trust with your partner is through eye contact. But eye contact can feel deeply vulnerable, which makes it more difficult than it sounds. Nonetheless, it's a useful trust-building tool because it keeps you focused and present during vulnerable conversations, and it helps increase awareness of physical cues and expressions.

1. Situate yourselves across from each other in a quiet space, without distractions.

2. While making eye contact, Partner A should share a simple statement that makes them feel fearful of being judged.

3. After Partner A has spoken, Partner B should respond with something along the lines of, "I hear that you sometimes feel . . . Is there anything I can do to help you with this fear/concern?"

4. Partner A can then share if there is anything Partner B can do to support them in this area. Then switch roles.

5. After you've both shared, fill in the blanks below.

PARTNER A

My partner talked about: _____

When they shared this, I felt: _____

When sharing my vulnerability, I felt: _____

PARTNER B

My partner talked about: _____

When they shared this, I felt: _____

When sharing my vulnerability, I felt: _____

Trust in the Future

Trust is something couples work on and maintain throughout the course and challenges of a relationship. At times, it will need repair and might require some flexibility. One effective way to service the trust in your relationship is to talk about your shared goals for the future. This exercise is designed to foster conversations about your values, hopes, and dreams.

1. Use the categories below to explore what your future might look like in ten years. You have complete permission to dream. In this case, do not worry about the "how" of it. Take a minute to imagine what your ultimate life looks like in the future and then share your dreams.

2. Do you have any conflicting hopes and dreams? Talk about them, and decide which are "must haves" and which are "nice to haves." Come to a consensus.

3. Fill in each category with a description of how you envision your shared lives to be. This exercise may entail some compromise.

RELATIONSHIPS
(Family and Friends)

CAREER AND FINANCE

WELL-BEING
(Emotional, Physical, or Spiritual)

FUN AND RECREATION

Affirming the Positives

Most people have negative thoughts from time to time, which is normal. But when those thoughts are not grounded in fact, they are called "thought distortions," and they can lead you to interpret neutral behaviors from your partner in a negative light. This exercise is designed to help you develop positive affirmations to challenge negative thoughts.

Each partner should identify three personal positive affirmations (e.g., "I am fully deserving of trust and respect."). Share your affirmations with each other by documenting them on the lines below. Take turns to help each other understand why you both chose your affirmations and document them on the corresponding "takeaway" line.

PARTNER A

Affirmation 1: ....

Affirmation 2: ....

Affirmation 3: ....

Takeaway 1: ....

Takeaway 2: ....

Takeaway 3: ....

PARTNER B

Affirmation 1: ....

Affirmation 2: ....

Affirmation 3: ....

Takeaway 1: ....

Takeaway 2: ....

Takeaway 3: ....

Commitment to Trust

Trust is critical both to building and maintaining a relationship. It requires vulnerability and accountability from both of you. In working through this chapter, you've already demonstrated a commitment to strengthening trust. The pledge is your chance to firm up plans to continue putting actions to your commitment.

1. Choose to do an activity together that requires both of you to take a risk and get out of your comfort zone. For example, attempting a new craft, taking a yoga class, or visiting an unknown part of town together.

2. Before you do the activity, get together and create a pledge to commit to trust in your relationship. First, each partner should write down a detailed statement about how they plan to accomplish this (e.g., "I pledge to reassure you that my love and friendship are yours even in conflict.").

3. After that, write a shared statement of commitment to trust together.

4. Make the pledges to each other and revisit this page as needed as a reminder of your commitments.

PARTNER A

I pledge to: ....

....

PARTNER B

I pledge to: ....

....

OUR SHARED PLEDGE

Together we pledge to: ....

....

....

CHAPTER 4

Communicate Effectively

With effective communication, good things happen. Each partner feels heard, validated, and valued. Talking and communicating are two different things, however. Talking is simply an expression of words linked together to relay a message. Communicating is an exchange that requires talking, and all of the non-verbal forms of expression that go with it, along with listening, hearing, and feedback. This chapter offers tools to optimize the communication between you and your partner, and the opportunity to practice using them. You will have the chance to take measure of your communication now and establish how you would like it to be in the future. The exercises will help you improve the effectiveness of your communication by looking at factors that break communication down and realizing your strengths.

How Effectively Do We Communicate?

In order to improve your communication, you need a clear assessment of where you stand today. This quiz measures your communication effectiveness and offers a way to discuss how to move forward.

Complete the quiz together, being as honest as possible. If you disagree, make sure you are both comfortable with your answer before circling a final one. When you are finished, add up your points and use the answer key at the end of the quiz to see where you stand. Use this exercise as a jumping-off point to discuss any changes you might want to make moving forward.

1. How quickly do you come together to talk about an area or topic of conflict after it occurs?
   a. Wait more than twenty-four hours
   b. Wait twenty-four hours
   c. Wait until that evening
   d. Wait a few hours
   e. Don't wait

2. How often do you talk about your plans, dreams, and aspirations?
   a. Never
   b. Almost never
   c. Sometimes
   d. Almost always
   e. Always

3. When you talk, what do you talk about most?
   a. Your household(s)
   b. Family and friends
   c. Short-term plans
   d. Dreams
   e. The future

4. Do you avoid communicating because you fear judgment or criticism?
   a. Yes, always
   b. Yes, most of the time
   c. Yes, sometimes
   d. No, not often
   e. No, never

5. What happens if you both have trouble coming to resolution?

    a. We remember and bring it up later.

    b. There is a lot of silence and passive aggressiveness.

    c. We agree to disagree, and move on.

    d. We hear each other's point of view and take time apart to think about it.

    e. We take a break in communication and come back to it later.

6. What is your primary intention when communicating?

    a. To win

    b. To prove I am right

    c. To pretend I am listening

    d. To be kind

    e. To listen to what my partner has to say

7. How often is accountability a part of your conflict resolution?

    a. Never

    b. Rarely

    c. Sometimes

    d. Often

    e. Always

SCORING: ■ A=5 ■ B=4 ■ C=3 ■ D=2 ■ E=1

ANSWER KEY

28–35 points: You've got to start somewhere. You have some work to do on more effective communication and committing to resolution in conflict. Don't be afraid to seek out help from a professional, if needed.

20–27 points: Let's focus on doing better. Although you do some things well, there is still a lot of room for improvement. Make a plan by identifying where improvements need to happen.

11–19 points: Doing pretty well, but there's always room for improvement. It looks like you've done some work in most areas, so keep the momentum going.

Less than 10 points: Communication is your super power. It's always a good idea to keep refining communication skills, but it seems like you've got a fantastic foundation.

The "Look" of Good Communication

Effective communication is key to getting what you need from a relationship. It allows each of you to share your experiences and inform each other about your needs in a way they can be heard. In addition, it encourages each partner to be vulnerable, take accountability when necessary, empathize, and get support. According to research from Drs. John and Julie Gottman, effective communication is void of criticism, defensiveness, contempt, and stonewalling. With ineffective communication in play, you will surely experience misunderstandings, strain, and possibly hostility.

1. In the "Now" box provided, draw something that represents how communication in your relationship currently feels. If there is some criticism, defensiveness, contempt, or stonewalling, how could you depict that?

2. Next, in the "Goal" box, draw how improved communication could look to you. For example, you might draw a porcupine with long, sharp quills to represent your communication patterns now and a porcupine that has shed its quills to reflect your goal.

3. Share your thoughts with your partner on why you chose your "Now" and "Goal" images and what it means to you to change some of the ways that you currently communicate.

PARTNER A

Now	Goal

PARTNER B

Now	Goal

Criticism Hurts

Feedback, no matter how well-intended, can sometimes turn into criticism. And when you receive criticism from your partner, it can feel much like an attack, causing you to react defensively. This is a common response and usually ends in unproductive communication, which can lead to feelings of not being heard or validated. This exercise will guide you to rephrase criticism that once halted communication into something that encourages open communication.

1. Select one common, frequent criticism that you both tend to use.

2. One of you will take the lead and write down the criticism as it appears in your communication now (e.g., "You always call me and cancel plans for last-minute stuff with your family.").

3. Criticism: _____

4. Turn this "attack" into a more reflective expression using the template below.

5. When you are finished, use this as a template to talk through another two or three common criticisms from each of you. If time allows, discuss the feelings you expressed with empathy.

I feel _____ (*fill in with feeling descriptor using words in the word bank below or using your*

own words) when _____ (*fill in with a description of the situation*).

Do you think you could _____ (*ask for what you need*)?

WORD BANK

Disappointed   Judged   Sad   Resentful   Frustrated

Confused   Annoyed   Neglected   Unimportant   Lonely

Ignored   Taken aback

Do You Hear the Way I Feel?

Giving your partner feedback is necessary when their behavior is affecting you negatively. The question is how to do it effectively. Instead of communicating what your partner is doing wrong in a critical way, share the feedback by helping your partner understand the way their behavior makes you feel. This exercise, as an adjunct to Criticism Hurts (page 41), will help both of you: Practice leading with your feelings rather than using critical blanket statements; focus on the behavior's impact on you; and avoid extreme generalizations using always/never framing.

1. Partner A: Choose a feelings adjective from the word bank.

2. Partner A: Use that adjective to express the way you have felt to your partner (e.g., "I feel lonely when you …").

3. Partner B: Validate or take accountability (e.g., "I hear that you feel lonely when I …").

4. Repeat with the roles reversed. Partner B can choose a new adjective or the same one.

WORD BANK

Frustrated　Overwhelmed　Excluded　Disappointed

Sad　Annoyed　Embarrassed　Jealous　Lonely

Stressed　Hurt　Worried

Becoming Less Defensive

When it comes to tough conversations or conflict, it is important to approach it not as coming to the mat to wrestle over victory but like coming to the table to find compromise. The reality is that if one partner feels or perceives they are being attacked, they are likely to respond defensively. Defensiveness is a way of protecting oneself from a valid or assumed criticism or judgment. Instead of getting defensive in the face of a perceived attack, you can:

- *Identify* the possible internal feeling your partner is experiencing that is causing them to be critical (e.g., "It sounds like me working late makes you feel lonely.").

- *Ask* your partner how the behavior they have criticized makes them feel (e.g., "How do you feel when I come home later than I said without calling?").

Following these steps will help you practice these alternative responses when feeling defensive.

1. Practice deep breathing together. Face each other and hold hands. Close your eyes and inhale for a count of four and out for a count of four. Repeat ten times.

2. Fill out the table below to think of less defensive responses to criticism. An example is provided.

CRITICISM	DEFENSIVE RESPONSE	PREFERRED RESPONSE
Why can't you just pick up your mess?	*Your closet is a mess too!*	*It sounds like me not picking up after myself is frustrating for you.*

Being Made to "Feel Small" Is Unacceptable

Sarcasm, eye rolling, and mocking are just a few of the invalidating behaviors that close off productive conversation. They suggest that one person is judging rather than listening and respecting. But not everyone realizes when they've gone to a judgmental place or that they are displaying these behaviors. In this exercise, work together to identify ways these behaviors may show up in your partnership, so you can recognize and avoid them going forward.

1. Together, populate the first column below with examples of any verbal or non-verbal expressions used in your partnership that have made you feel unappreciated, unheard, or disrespected. When your partner mentions something you do, try not to deny or defend the behavior. Just listen.

2. Reflect on whether there are common themes, like phrases that make one of you feel less-than in your accomplishments.

3. For each behavior you have identified, talk to each other to identify better ways that each of you could have received the message, and write them in the second column. Focus on getting the message heard and not on what is right or wrong.

INVALIDATING EXPRESSIONS	ALTERNATIVE RESPONSE

Listening with Intention

Listening is a learned skill. Often people "listen" while distracted or while trying to think of a response. This can make the other person feel dismissed. In effective communication, listening actually entails *active* listening: receiving verbal and non-verbal communication and then providing appropriate feedback that demonstrates understanding. The exercise that follows enhances your active listening skills.

1. Partner A will begin as the presenter, taking five minutes to talk about something important to them in the relationship.

2. When the five minutes are over, the listening partner will summarize what they heard their partner express about their feelings, thoughts, or needs. Don't start writing until after Partner A is finished speaking.

3. Repeat, switching roles.

4. When both of you have completed the exercise, take time to read your entries out loud, and make sure your partner took away the message you intended.

PARTNER A

I heard you express:

_____

_____

_____

PARTNER B

I heard you express:

_____

_____

_____

Taking Time Out

During disagreements, a part of the neural system in your brain called the amygdala can be activated, causing you to engage in a "fight or flight" response. You may find yourself feeling combative or just wanting to escape or shut down. Taking time to reset and doing some mindful activities at this time in your conflict is completely acceptable and even recommended. The most effective and compassionate way to do this is to inform your partner of what is going on for you internally. Use expressions like, "I'm feeling overwhelmed right now. Can we revisit this conversation in twenty minutes?" Engage in the word search as a fun way to begin a conversation about ways to handle communication when one of you feels overwhelmed.

1. Read a word below and its description together, then find and circle it in the word search on page 47. (Words are hidden vertically, horizontally, and diagonally.) Continue until you have found all the words.

2. When completed, talk about alternative ways you can handle things when communication becomes too much to handle and one of you wants to shut it down. Identify the word search terms that you feel will be most and least effective for your communication with one another.

Empathy: Search for understanding of your partner's emotions and support them with love.

Availability: Tell your partner you are free to talk whenever they are ready.

Connect: It is okay to take a pause from the conversation and do something you both enjoy.

Communicate: Don't meet a shut down with a shut down. Instead lean into your effective communication with an open mind and positive non-verbal affirmation.

Toe-to-Toe: Fight the urge to match the energy of your partner when they shut down. Matched negative energy will only escalate the situation.

Self-Care: Stress in the relationship can be intensified if you are not taking care of yourself physically and mentally, leading to more difficult conflict resolution. Take care of yourselves.

Pardon: Show your partner some grace and excuse them from past complaints.

G	G	B	K	Z	N	U	F	F	K	G	T	I	G	A
C	Z	I	Y	V	L	S	D	W	W	F	X	T	R	V
U	K	T	H	F	C	U	A	H	X	E	C	L	Z	A
Q	T	O	A	A	A	M	Y	N	Q	E	P	F	S	I
C	X	E	U	X	M	Q	Q	M	N	B	N	Q	C	L
X	D	T	C	O	M	M	U	N	I	C	A	T	E	A
X	A	O	C	R	P	F	O	F	S	Q	Q	Q	I	B
Z	S	T	U	I	C	C	W	G	E	I	C	P	N	I
A	B	O	P	X	D	P	G	V	G	F	O	O	L
Q	W	E	Q	O	W	T	C	D	F	N	D	F	J	I
Y	U	P	W	N	J	I	F	I	C	R	V	F	Y	T
E	M	P	A	T	H	Y	F	D	A	N	P	Y	Q	Y
R	R	N	P	C	S	T	U	P	R	D	V	V	Y	Y
K	C	O	I	G	L	R	F	P	E	S	J	N	I	U
A	T	H	G	N	X	G	F	H	O	N	M	H	G	H

WORD BANK

Empathy   Availability   Connect   Communicate

Toe-to-toe   Self-Care   Pardon

I Love You, But . . .

Because you are humans in personal relationships, things will not always be perfect. There will be times when you get irritated by something your partner does or says. These may be pet peeves. This exercise has you communicate your recurring minor irritations with each other in order to gain a better understanding of the way your partner's actions make you feel.

Document and communicate your identified pet peeve for your partner in the space provided. Try your best to avoid sounding critical by using these steps:

1. Let your partner know how the pet peeve makes you feel (e.g., frustrated, annoyed).

2. State the pet peeve without pointing a finger at them literally or verbally. Say it rationally (e.g., "When there is water on the bathroom counter, I often get my clothes wet before going to work.").

3. Ask for what you need (e.g., "Can you please check for water on the counter after you brush your teeth?").

PARTNER A

My pet peeve:

How it makes me feel:

The change I would like to see:

PARTNER B

My pet peeve: ....

....

....

How it makes me feel: ....

....

....

The change I would like to see: ....

....

....

Being Mindful

Actively listening to your partner requires the ability to grasp their words, their non-verbal cues, and the intended meaning of both. This takes great scrutiny and can be difficult at times. To gain focus and center before having difficult conversations, it can be helpful to clear your head mindfully. This exercise will help you both to slow down and relax so that you can take in what your partner is trying to communicate.

1. Find a quiet space to sit down together for ten to fifteen minutes.

2. Sit comfortably across from each other, hold hands, and take deep breaths simultaneously, in through your nose and out through your mouth.

3. Notice how your breath feels as you inhale and exhale.

4. If you are holding any tension, imagine it leaving your body as you exhale.

5. Take turns reciting the following pledge to one another:

    I am loved. We are enough.

    Our mistakes do not define us.

    We will do our best to hear one another.

    We are allowed to set boundaries and expect others to respect them.

6. When you are finished, notice what you feel and take turns discussing one thing that has been on your mind or is a source of stress in your relationship.

Commitment to Effective Communication

As you continue to grow together, you may find that effective communication heals wounds and increases your connection. Remember that communication takes two, and you are both works in progress. The pledge is a commitment to keep getting better together every day and a reminder on your way to communicating with honesty and vulnerability.

1. Choose a date and time to have a meal together in the next week.

2. Before the meal, meet and read the pledge. Use the lines underneath to customize it to your own relationship.

3. Make the pledge to each other. Then seal it by enjoying your meal together.

4. Revisit this pledge often as a reminder of your commitment.

COMMUNICATION PLEDGE

I pledge to make an effort to communicate better. I want to feel heard, and I want to give you the opportunity to understand me better as well. It is not my intention to hurt, dismiss, or criticize you. If my words do so, please let me know. I will do better. I am here for you and to validate your thoughts. I love you.

CHAPTER 5

Establish Respect

Respect is one expression of love within your relationship. Respect means truly appreciating your differences. It means thoughtfully valuing who your partner is, recognizing their worth and their unique qualities. It takes work to continually hold your partner's uniqueness in your relationship in high esteem. But that work pays itself back tenfold. Genuine mutual respect leads to increased connectedness, trust, and the ability to be vulnerable in your relationship. Use the exercises in this chapter to reflect on what respect looks like for each of you as individuals and to learn how to establish, maintain, and bolster respect between you as a couple.

What Is Respect to You?

Respect is often difficult to define, but you absolutely know when it is absent. You may feel disrespected when your partner does not give you the same consideration that they might expect for themselves, causing resentment. For this reason, you and your partner need to discuss and establish at the outset what mutual respect in your relationship looks like. What is respect to you? To your partner?

Take turns filling in the blank spaces with different endings to the two sentences. Then talk through why you felt that way.

PARTNER A

I feel respected when: ....

I feel disrespected when: ....

I feel respected when: ....

I feel disrespected when: ....

PARTNER B

I feel respected when: ....

I feel disrespected when: ....

I feel respected when: ....

I feel disrespected when: ....

How Does Respect Show Up?

Respect requires understanding, valuing, listening, encouraging, giving, apologizing, accepting responsibility, and so much more. Use this exercise to assess how you demonstrate respect for one another and to determine if there are areas where you could show more.

Use the table to document the ways and places respect already shows up in your relationship; also document opportunity areas where respect can be improved. For each area, decide together and discuss the rationale for which column to choose. Then, plan to address the areas that fall under "area for improvement." Feel free to add your own areas for respect as well.

AREA OF RESPECT	HOW IT SHOWS UP NOW	AREA FOR IMPROVEMENT
Listening to each other's points of view		
Valuing each other's opinions/advice		
Giving each other full attention when in conversation		
Encouraging each other to succeed equally		
Apologizing when one partner has made the other feel badly (even when it was unintended)		
Allowing each other the space to socialize individually		

Respect Then and Now

How you show respect can differ depending on relationship dynamics. Showing respect to an elder or an authority figure might look and feel very different than the respect you show or receive from friends or romantic partners. And everyone's experience with, and expectations for, the way respect is given differ based on childhood experiences. This exercise will help each of you understand the role and meaning of respect in your lives from different perspectives. With greater understanding comes greater connection.

1. Separately, in the lines provided, identify three roles you identify with (e.g., child, niece/nephew, student, athlete, partner, parent). In the box with each identity, describe the expectations you were taught about respect in each role (e.g., As a child, I showed respect by addressing adults as "sir" and "ma'am.").

2. Also, document the similarities and differences between the types of respect you demonstrated for the different roles.

3. Reflecting on how respect exists in other areas of your life, work *together* to decide on and write down expectations for the way you'd like respect to look and feel within your relationship.

4. Finally, create and write down a plan for how you will monitor and maintain respect in your relationship going forward.

PARTNER A

Role 1: ....

Role 2: ....

Role 3: ....

How is respect the same across the roles? ....

....

How is respect different across the roles? ....

....

Role 1: ....

Role 2: ....

Role 3: ....

How is respect the same across the roles? ....

....

How is respect different across the roles? ....

....

RESPECT IN OUR RELATIONSHIP

How we want respect to look and feel in our relationship:

....

....

....

....

Our plan to monitor and maintain respect in our relationship:

....

....

....

....

Respect Is Music to My Ears

Conversations regarding mutual respect and disrespect can get tense because the stakes feel high and finding the right words can be difficult. These high stakes can cause stress; this is where music can come to the rescue. Music increases dopamine in your brain, leading to feelings of pleasure and love, both helpful in building and strengthening your relationship. In this exercise, you will use the lyrics in your favorite music to communicate your expectations for respect. When you finish, each of you will have a deeper understanding of how your partner interprets and feels respect in your relationship.

1. Each partner should research and identify song lyrics that best describe their feelings on respect.

2. Document the lyrics that are most relatable and your description of why you relate to them so well in the lines provided.

3. Take turns sharing your thoughts with your partner, then play them the full song.

PARTNER A

Song lyrics that describe respect for me:

I chose this song because:

PARTNER B

Song lyrics that describe respect for me:

I chose this song because:

Feelings and Thoughts around Disrespect

One common response to feeling disrespected is to internalize it, directing the negative thoughts and feelings inward. This can take a toll on self-esteem. This exercise is designed to help you recognize this cycle by working together to determine areas where each of you feels disrespect, resulting in negative feelings; talking about these feelings can prevent and/or remedy the underlying causes of the disrespect.

1. Have a robust discussion to identify three main areas in your relationship where each of you feels a sense of disrespect.

2. Take turns talking about each one and the negative feelings and thoughts that you internalize as a result. A negative feeling might be "irritated," or a thought might be something like, "You don't think my opinion matters." Document your findings below.

3. Afterwards, share with each other how the exercise felt, and commit to repeating it in the future when faced with similar situations.

	PARTNER A	PARTNER B
Areas of Disrespect	Negative Thoughts and Feelings	Negative Thoughts and Feelings

Do You Know My Passion?

One way to demonstrate respect for your partner is by showing interest in and understanding of your partner's passions in life. That could mean asking continual exploratory questions and taking time to listen actively to each other's responses. What both partners see as their individual passions and areas of interest can change over time, so keep up and keep asking regularly. Equally important to being aware of your partner's interests is encouraging them. This activity will give you some insight into each other's passions in life, any fears that are getting in the way, and what they need from you to get them closer to their goals.

1. Take turns asking each other about your passions in life and what, if anything, you want to do with that passion (e.g., "My passion is luxury cars, and I want to work to buy my own dealership.").

2. Document what you hear your partner express as their passion and any related goals, their fears around that goal, and what they need from you.

3. Then switch roles.

PARTNER A

My passion is: ....

My goal(s) for my passion is: ....

What I need from my partner: ....

PARTNER B

My passion is: ....

My goal(s) for my passion is: ....

What I need from my partner: ....

Sharing Professional Hopes and Dreams

Respect is often relayed by expressed interest in your partner's life, including, but not limited to, their occupation. Work is one of the main time commitments in day-to-day life. Having your partner show interest in something that impactful for you leads to a deeper level of connection in your relationship. This applies to partners who run the home as well as partners who work outside of the home. For that reason, it is important to understand, keep up with, and value your partner's work life objectives. In this exercise, you will each share your vision of how work will look for you in the future; by sharing, you will be able to understand and support each other in reaching your individual career goals.

1. Partner A can begin by sharing a narrative about what they do for work now, what they want to be doing in five years, and what they want to be doing in ten years.

2. Partner B should document their partner's plans using the timeline below.

3. Switch roles.

4. Discuss how your plans do or do not align by comparing your timelines. Document your collective findings about your plans and any ideas or realizations. This will be your collective plan. Make sure to refer to it regularly to talk through necessary adjustments over time.

PARTNER A

Now	In Five Years	In Ten Years

PARTNER B

Now	In Five Years	In Ten Years

OUR SHARED PLANS:

I Know You So Well . . . or Do I?

When people first meet, they tend to ask questions to get to know each other. These can cover everything from the past to their dreams for the future. As time goes on, couples tend to stop being so inquisitive. But there is always more to learn. Interest in and a desire to learn more about your partner is an obvious way to demonstrate respect for them. This exercise will help you return to the joy of exploration and the celebration of what makes you both unique.

1. On a separate sheet of paper, answer each of the questions about your partner listed on the opposite page.

2. Go through each question, telling your partner how you think they would answer the question. Take one question at a time.

   a. If you are correct, write it in the space provided.

   b. If incorrect, have your partner share the correct answer with you and write that down in the space provided.

3. Talk about what you learned about each other and how you felt about this depth of information.

4. Finally, in conversation, share a final piece of information about yourself that your partner may not know.

	PARTNER A	PARTNER B
Who is your partner's favorite family member?		
What does your partner admire about you?		
What is your partner's favorite animal?		
What is making your partner most stressed right now?		
If money weren't an issue, how would your partner spend their time?		
What is your partner's earliest memory?		
What does your partner need from you when they get sick?		
What is your partner's favorite movie?		
If your partner could dine with anyone (living or dead), who would it be?		

You Will Make Mistakes, but Please Own It

Accountability, or accepting responsibility for your actions, is a part of respect in a relationship. Although it's not reasonable to promise each other perfection, you can commit to owning up to mistakes when they do happen. Accountability is about taking ownership of your own actions and choices in the midst of conflict with one another. Without it, there is no acknowledgement of any negative impact of choices, and the blame for the conflict lies with only one partner. Practice taking responsibility with this exercise by learning the difference between expressions of accountability and more unreliable or dismissive responses.

1. Together, brainstorm various statements that you agree demonstrate respect and accountability. Think back to recent instances when one of you shared your feelings or thoughts on a difficult situation. What phrases sounded like taking responsibility?

2. Next, talk through examples of responses in your conflict where you felt like your partner was not taking their fair share of responsibility.

3. Talk about how it felt for each of you to hear each type of statement.

4. Commit to using phrases that sound like genuine accountability to both of you.

EXPRESSIONS OF ACCOUNTABILITY

■ *Example: It sounds like I made you feel like you weren't a priority, and I'm sorry.*

■ ....

■ ....

■ ....

UNRELIABLE OR DISMISSIVE EXPRESSIONS

■ *Example: I'm sorry you felt that way.*

■ ....

■ ....

■ ....

Meeting in the Middle with Understanding

The road to understanding starts with listening. Actively listening to your partner can entail putting yourself in their shoes for the moment. You don't have to agree with your partner's point of view to genuinely try to understand and validate it. You can start by acknowledging and rephrasing what they've said. This exercise will challenge you to take a topic and practice validating each other's point of view.

1. Together, select a topic for debate on which you have opposing opinions.

2. Decide on one partner to act as scribe. Using the blank Venn diagram, list your opposing views in the left and right hand sides of the diagram. List any areas on which you agree in the middle of the diagram.

3. Now, focus on the points that fall outside the center of the diagram.

4. Validate your partner's thoughts on these items by listening to understand; acknowledging your partner's feelings, opinions, and thoughts; and rephrasing to make sure your partner knows you listened and understood.

5. If possible, notice whether any of the items can move to the center. But remember, this should not be the ultimate goal. You are not trying to persuade one another; the purpose is to feel understood.

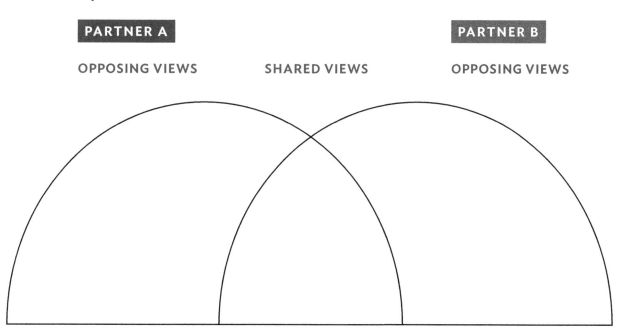

PARTNER A　　　　　　　　　　　　　　　　　　**PARTNER B**

OPPOSING VIEWS　　　　SHARED VIEWS　　　　OPPOSING VIEWS

Commitment to Respect

This is a pledge to offer each other mutual respect in your relationship. Treat each other with thoughtful consideration, and provide each other with a safe space by honoring your individual boundaries, differences, thoughts, and feelings. The pledge is an opportunity to put guided action to your commitment to practicing mutual respect in your relationship.

1. Schedule an outside activity you both enjoy.

2. Before the activity, get together and read the pledge. Use the lines underneath to customize it for your relationship, if you wish. Document anything else you commit to regarding mutual respect.

3. When on your date or immediately before, officially make the pledge to each other. It is all right to take this pledge often as a reminder of your commitment to mutual respect.

A PLEDGE OF RESPECT

I pledge to do my very best to respect your boundaries, your feelings, and your thoughts. I will acknowledge and respect your hopes and dreams and validate your plans for the future. When I do not come through on this, I will appreciate your grace as we grow together. Through this act of kindness, I will show my love for you.

CHAPTER 6

Create Healthy Boundaries

Sometimes the word "boundaries" gets a bad rap because setting boundaries can be awkward. But the benefits are so much greater than the discomfort. Boundaries are limits you set to protect your well-being. Each partner in a relationship has the right to decide what they are comfortable with and what expectations they hold when it comes to, among other things: physical space, personal belongings, emotional needs, privacy, and time. It is necessary to set a boundary when either of you feels uncomfortable in a situation. It's up to each of you to determine the source of your own discomfort and then communicate your feelings and what you need to feel more comfortable. Ultimately, creating healthy boundaries between partners enhances trust. This chapter offers exercises to help you assess the boundaries you have in your relationship, determine where some healthy boundaries may help improve your trust, and create boundaries in a positive and effective manner.

Unhealthy Boundaries Bring On Negative Feelings

A relationship with healthy boundaries holds regard for both partners' needs, values, and limits. But when boundaries do not exist, the partner needing boundaries can start to feel resentful, unheard, or unappreciated. This activity will help you structure and practice boundary-setting.

Take a look at the list of feelings below. Circle the three (or add your own) that are most familiar to you as they relate to the relationship you have with your partner. Then complete the statements that follow with your chosen feeling words, situations that tend to bring them up, and a description of the boundary that may help mitigate the negative feelings.

WORD BANK

Frustrated   Resentful   Overwhelmed   Confused

Skeptical   Jealous   Sad   Anxious   Stupid

Other:_____   Other:_____   Other:_____

PARTNER A

I feel _____ when my partner does this: _____. What I need is

_____.

I feel _____ when my partner does this: _____. What I need is

_____.

PARTNER B

I feel _____ when my partner does this: _____. What I need is

_____.

I feel _____ when my partner does this: _____. What I need is

_____.

Why Boundaries Are Difficult

This exercise will help you understand some of the reasons why you may be hesitant or unable to set boundaries so that you can break through and establish the effective limitations needed to enhance your relationship.

First, think about a specific situation in your relationship where you felt the need for a boundary but were hesitant to set one. How did it feel for you? Share your individual perspectives with one another. Next, document the reasons you've felt in the past for not setting boundaries in your relationships (for example, a desire to people please, a fear of rejection, second-guessing yourself, or fear of a negative reaction). When you have completed the table, talk to each other to clarify your reasons for not setting boundaries in the different types of relationships.

PARTNER A

Reasons for Not Setting Boundaries in My Relationship	Reasons for Not Setting Boundaries with Friends and Family

PARTNER B

Reasons for Not Setting Boundaries in My Relationship	Reasons for Not Setting Boundaries with Friends and Family

The Art of Restating "No"

Your "no" is important and should be respected, full stop. But it's not the only way to set a firm boundary in your relationship. You may consider starting a boundary-setting statement with words like "I want," "I need," or "I expect." This approach signals that you are trying to set a limit, and at the same time lets your partner into your thought process. This exercise will let you practice and create boundary-setting statements that feel good in your interactions. Nonetheless, it is important to respect boundaries no matter what package they may come in.

Get together and brainstorm various ways to express your boundaries respectfully instead of a straightforward "no." Use specific examples from your interactions. These should be ways that each partner can hear limitations without taking offense. Practice by using statements that begin with: "I want," "I need," or "I expect."

After practice, document the ways that you both have agreed are workable options.

Different Boundaries for Different Spaces

Generally, your boundaries are set expectations that make you feel safe and comfortable. Setting boundaries removes discomfort in situations but requires that you be vulnerable enough to share how these situations make you feel in the first place. Remember, boundaries in your relationship are defined by *you*. This exercise will help you think about the various areas of your life where boundaries may need to be put into place so that you both feel safe enough to be vulnerable.

1. Working together, consider which of the areas below you feel you would benefit from more detailed boundaries.

2. Use the "Other" spaces to add areas that you think might benefit from boundaries in your relationship.

3. Then decide what specific boundaries might look like for each of you. Write these down in the "Desired Boundaries" column.

4. Keep in mind that this is not a final determination of boundaries, but rather a start to the conversation.

AREA	DESIRED BOUNDARIES
Personal time	
Personal space	
Shared responsibilities/ chores	
Involvement with friends/ family	
Other:	
Other:	

The How-To of Setting Boundaries

There will be times in any relationship when communicating your needs will be difficult. You may be stifled by concern of it having a negative impact on your relationship. It is important to a healthy relationship, however, that you find a way to communicate your boundaries in a way that your partner can hear them. This exercise encourages you to use boundary-setting dialogue tailored to your own unique relationship.

1. Together, review the phrases below that can be used to set boundaries in your relationship.

2. Circle the boundary-setting phrases that most clearly signal a limit or boundary in your relationship.

3. Use the additional lines provided to add your own boundary-setting phrases or words.

4. For each one circled or added, walk through examples in your lives together that apply.

BOUNDARY-SETTING PHRASES

I'm uncomfortable . . .

I don't want to . . .

Maybe we should . . .

I need you to stop . . .

No . . .

I want . . .

I expect . . .

Other: _____

Other: _____

Other: _____

Sexual Boundaries

As with many aspects of a relationship, the role of sex is influenced by your unique experiences and preferences. This extends to setting boundaries on things such as frequency, verbal interaction, touch, and other acts that are either preferred or off-limits. By completing the grid below, you will explore sexual boundaries with each other openly, honestly, and nonjudgmentally. When your practices feel safe to both partners, they create space for greater satisfaction.

Each partner should fill out one column. Use the space to get as specific as you would like about each boundary. Feel free to use pen; you do not have to change these boundaries for your partner. Be sure to listen to your partner with respect and avoid being critical of their boundaries.

	PARTNER A	PARTNER B
Frequency boundaries		
Touch boundaries		
Position boundaries		
Verbal expression boundaries		
Other:		
Other:		

The Meaning Behind Our Money

Money is a frequent tension point. But as with other aspects of your relationship, setting boundaries around finances will lead to respectful communication based on the needs of each partner. For example, you could set boundaries related to the level of transparency around finances, budgeting processes, and spending limits. In this exercise, you will explore boundaries and thoughts about finances and then set financial goals together.

1. Each partner should answer each question provided. For each answer, consider whether you need to talk about a boundary. (For example, "As a child, my family never had enough money for necessities because my dad spent too much on things he wanted. I need to set a budget to make sure we have covered our necessities before putting money aside for miscellaneous expenditures.")

2. Validate your partner's answers and ask open-ended questions to get more depth. (For example, "It sounds like you are comfortable sharing your expenses but not your income. Can you help me understand what your income means to you?")

3. After completing the question-and-answer portion, use what you've learned to create joint financial goals. Consider topics like paying down debt, saving for retirement, saving for something specific, or investments. Document these goals and come back to review them as often as you need.

FINANCIAL QUESTIONS

What did you learn about money as a kid? How did your caregivers treat money?

Partner A:

Partner B:

Did your family talk about money openly?

Partner A:

Partner B:

Do you feel a responsibility to support anyone besides yourself financially?

Partner A:

Partner B:

What does having money mean to you?

Partner A: ....

Partner B: ....

Did you ever struggle with money?

Partner A: ....

Partner B: ....

What are your feelings about debt?

Partner A: ....

Partner B: ....

What do you allow yourself to splurge on? What splurge would you never give up?

Partner A: ....

Partner B: ....

What does retirement look like to you?

Partner A: ....

Partner B: ....

OUR SHARED FINANCIAL GOALS

1. ....
2. ....
3. ....
4. ....
5. ....

Keeping Friends and Family in Our Lives but Out of Our Business

For many couples, feedback from friends and family can be helpful in shaping their relationships. At times, it can be less helpful. Listen to advice from those you admire, and then discuss it with your partner to determine your desire to incorporate the advice. This boundary-setting will ensure you consider your partner's boundaries as well as your own. This exercise will have you explore the level of involvement you are willing to accept from friends and family.

1. Together, discuss family and friends who are more generous with their feedback and advice.

2. In the "In Scope" section of the circle, write down any areas of your life in which you are both receptive to advice from these people.

3. In the "Out of Scope" section of the circle, write down any areas of your life that you want to try to handle on your own or keep private.

4. When you are done, discuss areas that a friend or family member has been violating. Think about a plan to talk to them about your boundary and discuss the wording. You might like to create a phrase in which you thank them for their input then use clear boundary-setting phrases such as "I need," "I expect," or "I want."

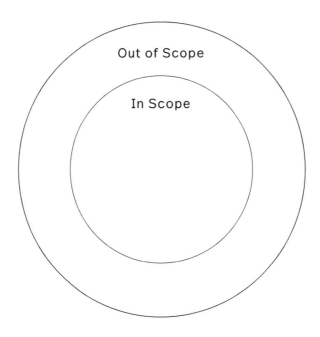

Your Support Systems

Being in a relationship does not diminish the value of fulfilling friendships and support systems. Use the space provided to establish time allocations for what is important in your lives, including, but not limited to, time together, time with friends, family time, and time for self-care.

PARTNER A

SUN	
MON	
TUE	
WED	
THU	
FRI	
SAT	

PARTNER B

SUN	
MON	
TUE	
WED	
THU	
FRI	
SAT	

A Helping Hand in Building Boundaries

Setting boundaries is important to the strength of your relationship. But it is also a necessary skill to manage friendships and family relationships. As partners, you can help each other set boundaries with others and hold each other accountable for maintaining the boundaries.

1. In the space provided, each partner should write down a person, outside of your relationship, with whom they would like to set a specific boundary.

2. Jot down the boundaries you would like to set, and refine the language together.

3. Make a commitment to support each other in keeping the specified boundary.

PARTNER A

Person with whom I want to set a boundary: ....

The boundary: ....

....

Support I need from my partner: ....

....

PARTNER B

Person with whom I want to set a boundary: ....

The boundary: ....

....

Support I need from my partner: ....

....

Commitment to Respecting Boundaries

This is a pledge that you will focus on respecting boundaries as a priority in your relationship. Plan to stay in and enjoy a meal together. It can be a romantic dinner or a refreshing brunch. Make it whatever you both enjoy most. Before your time together, individually complete the pledges provided. Be as specific as you can based on what you've learned about each other so far. After finishing your meal, give the pledge to each other.

BOUNDARY PLEDGES

PARTNER A I pledge to respect your boundaries and make you aware of mine. I recognize your primary boundary needs as:

....

....

....

I recognize that your boundaries may change, and I will give you the space to communicate them to me as they come.

PARTNER B I pledge to respect your boundaries and make you aware of mine. I recognize your primary boundary needs as:

....

....

....

I recognize that your boundaries may change, and I will give you the space to communicate them to me as they come.

CHAPTER 7

Healthy Conflict

You can handle differences of opinion in several ways. You can come to battle, looking for one winner. Or, you can come to the table to listen to each other and communicate your points of view. The latter will get you to a place of compromise where you can address and consider each other's thoughts and desires. The former tactic will leave one or both of you dissatisfied and foster a less healthy dynamic. This chapter offers tools to approach conflict by staying present, communicating respectfully, and using compromise, empathy, validation, and understanding. The tools themselves may seem simple, but using them in the moment during a conflict can be a challenge. Nonetheless, if you put in the effort, you can make them into positive habits.

Healthy Versus Unhealthy Conflict

Conflict in your relationship is natural and only demonstrates that you are comfortable sharing your opinion with your partner. In fact, if it is handled in a healthy way, it can lead to strengthened trust and, therefore, a deeper connectedness and understanding. When handled in an unhealthy manner, it can lead to distance and despair. Healthy conflict is identified by transparency, listening, validation, and compromise. Unhealthy conflict is void of one or more of these elements. This exercise exposes you to various conflict scenarios and asks you to identify if they are healthy or not. It will open a forum for you and your partner to talk through your expectations for future disagreements.

Begin by reading the two scenarios together. Then work together to label each scenario as healthy or unhealthy conflict, and check the reason(s) why from the list provided.

SCENARIO 1

You tell your partner that it seems like they always prefer to hang out with their friends when you have free time. Your partner takes a minute to think, and then says that they can see how you feel that way. Your partner asks that you say something the next time you have free time because they would prefer to spend time with you.

THIS SCENARIO IS AN EXAMPLE OF:

☐ Healthy Conflict ☐ Unhealthy Conflict

THIS IS DUE TO THE PRESENCE OR ABSENCE OF:

☐ Transparency ☐ Validation

☐ Listening ☐ Compromise

SCENARIO 2

Your partner wants to go to their family's house in another state for the holidays. You would prefer to go see your family nearby because you enjoy the traditions you are used to. But you tell your partner that you would rather not fly during the holidays. Your partner suggests you split the holidays, and you still refuse.

THIS SCENARIO IS AN EXAMPLE OF:

☐ Healthy Conflict   ☐ Unhealthy Conflict

THIS IS DUE TO THE PRESENCE OR ABSENCE OF:

☐ Transparency   ☐ Validation

☐ Listening   ☐ Compromise

Compromise Is Fair

Sometimes, conflict in your relationship may feel beyond resolution. But generally, this is not the case. Sometimes, reaching a resolution means compromising. This entails accepting that the best solution is not one or the other, but a third entirely different one. If both of you feel dissatisfied with the suggested compromise, it means you have both given too much and may need to revisit the situation for a better solution. When to compromise and when to hold your ground? That is for you to decide, but a general guideline is that compromise is not a good idea when either partner's needs are violated, when either partner feels disrespected, or when a compromise means stepping back from your identity or core values.

Reflect on a recent conflict about which you felt like you would never see eye to eye.

1. Fill in the circles with the things that are important to you in relation to the conflict. What are you advocating for? Then take a highlighter and highlight the things that you feel are deal breakers (needs). Leave your unhighlighted statements as "nice to haves."

2. Talk to your partner about the deal breakers and why they are so important to you. Ask your partner to validate your needs. Take turns.

3. Finally, in the "Our Resolution" space, write down all of your needs and your partner's needs. Then use these to begin a conversation on resolving the conflict.

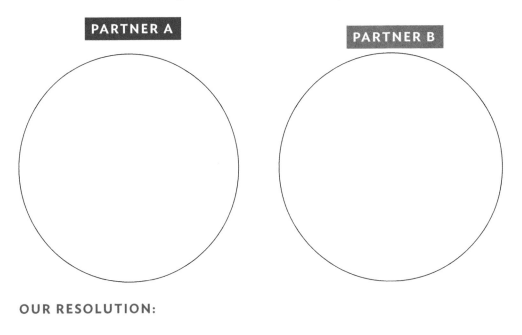

PARTNER A

PARTNER B

OUR RESOLUTION:

Active Listening

Active listening comes into play in so many areas of a healthy relationship. It builds trust, enhances communication, forges respect, is critical for setting boundaries, and is a major component of healthy conflict. After all, in order to truly hear and be heard in a disagreement, both parties must implement active listening skills, meaning paraphrasing, using open-ended questions, and reading/using non-verbal cues. It is through active listening that you build trust and connection in your relationship so that you can reach a resolution. This exercise will help you practice active listening and learn a little more about each other as a bonus.

1. Decide who will be the first talker and who will be the first listener.

2. Set a timer for three minutes.

3. The talker will speak on the topic of their choice for three minutes, uninterrupted.

4. When done, the listener will write down the top three points they heard during that time.

5. Switch roles and repeat.

PARTNER A

Top three talking points:

1. ....

2. ....

3. ....

PARTNER B

Top three talking points:

1. ....

2. ....

3. ....

When Heated, Take Time to Get Calm

Do you ever feel so passionate about your own point of view during a conflict that you feel like your insides are boiling? When you feel this anger, it is difficult to be fair, think clearly, or make good decisions, because the prefrontal cortex of your brain—the part that controls reasoning and judgment—is disengaged. In this exercise, you will practice deep breathing together in the absence of conflict so that you can work on getting and staying calm during conflict.

1. Put on some instrumental, calming music or soothing sounds.

2. Close your eyes and hold hands while facing one another.

3. Breathe in for five seconds and out for five seconds. Repeat ten times.

4. Start at the top of your head and scan your entire body, down to your toes. Notice the parts of your body that might be tense (shoulders, hands, stomach, etc.). When you feel a tense area, intentionally tighten it up, count to eight, and release it. Then move on to the next tense body part.

5. When you are finished, squeeze your partner's hands to let them know.

6. When both partners are done, together breathe in for five seconds and breathe out for five seconds. Repeat ten times.

7. Share how you felt during and after the exercise with your partner. Discuss how you can access this feeling in times of need.

The Value of Empathy in Conflict

Empathy is about showing that you understand your partner's experiences and emotions in each situation. It leads to feelings of trust and belonging. There are many ways to show empathy. You can imagine that you are experiencing the conflict in your partner's situation (e.g., "Yes, if I were you, I'd feel lonely too."). You can use a feeling word to communicate that you know how your partner feels (e.g., "I think what I hear you saying is that you felt lonely when I left you to talk to my friends."). You can even ask questions for understanding (e.g., "Are you saying that you felt lonely when you were left alone?"). In this exercise, you'll reflect on an emotional conflict you've had and practice various ways to react with empathy.

1. Discuss and review the details of the conflict so you are aligned.

2. Have Partner A express the way they feel about the topic of conflict. Have Partner B make note of how they feel, and write this in the space provided.

3. Have Partner B respond with three statements that convey their empathy, and write these in the space provided.

4. Switch roles and repeat.

PARTNER A

How my partner feels about the conflict:

Statement that conveys empathy #1:

Statement that conveys empathy #2:

Statement that conveys empathy #3:

PARTNER B

How my partner feels about the conflict:

Statement that conveys empathy #1:

Statement that conveys empathy #2:

Statement that conveys empathy #3:

Understanding Non-Verbal Communication in Conflict

Conflict has a verbal and non-verbal component. Sure, you get your points across using your words, but you might not even realize what your non-verbal communication is saying. Do your non-verbal cues match your words? Do you say, "I'm fine," but have your eyebrows scrunched up or your arms crossed? This exercise will help you understand how your partner is receiving your non-verbal communication. It will help you determine what is working for you and against you in conflict and in your communication generally.

1. Think back to a recent difficult conversation you had with each other. It might be easy to remember the narrative involved, but challenge yourselves to try to remember the non-verbal communication you received.

2. Use the table on the following page to talk through some of the different types of non-verbal communication you may have received from your partner during conflict. In the space provided, write down the way it made you feel or what it made you think.

3. Feel free to use the last few lines for other non-verbal cues.

   Note: This may be difficult. Remember to stay calm and open, and work as a team to refine this element of your communication.

NON-VERBALS	PARTNER A	PARTNER B
Crossed arms		
Unconscious shrug		
Rolling eyes		
Nodding head		
Wandering eyes		
Hand covering mouth		
Scrunched eyebrows		
Other:		
Other:		

The Harm of Accusations in Conflict

In conflict, one common defense mechanism or behavior is to levy criticism in order to make a point. It is crucial to keep in mind, however, that insults, hurtful words, and accusations can severely harm your relationship because they can stay in the air long after resolving the specific conflict. This exercise will take you back to a recent interaction where you either resorted to verbal attacks or felt verbally attacked by your partner. The purpose is to help you both develop new habits on which to draw rather than lashing out.

1. Describe the last time your partner said something during a conflict that made you feel hurt or dismissed. Be sure to explain why their words had that impact on you.

2. Pause for a minute or two to give each other space and time to take accountability.

3. Now take a moment to rephrase what you were originally trying to communicate without being critical or accusatory.

4. Conclude this activity by writing a statement of intent to make efforts to avoid accusatory language in the future. Try to make your intentions toward one another as specific as possible.

PARTNER A

I intend to:

_____

_____

PARTNER B

I intend to:

_____

_____

Reflection for Understanding

After conflict, it's possible that you will both feel lingering tension. This may be a sign that one or both of you is having trouble forgiving your partner for criticism or contempt present in the conflict. This exercise asks you to recall a recent incident and do some role-play to practice empathy, understanding, and forgiveness.

1. Partner A should identify a recent incident in which they felt hurt by their partner and write it on the line provided.

2. Now, Partner A, pretend you are in Partner B's role as the initiator of the hurtful action.

3. Partner B: Ask broad questions of Partner A, as if you are trying to better understand the incident. Imagine yourself in the role of needing to forgive.

4. Switch roles and repeat.

5. Complete the form below.

PARTNER A

The incident: _____

Why my partner may have behaved in that way: _____

What my partner may have felt: _____

What my partner could have done differently: _____

PARTNER B

The incident: _____

Why my partner may have behaved in that way: _____

What my partner may have felt: _____

What my partner could have done differently: _____

Perspective Sharing on Conflict

The ways you have seen people approach conflict in the past can affect how you address and resolve it in the present. For instance, if you've witnessed aggression, gaslighting, and passive aggression in the face of conflict, you may not be as familiar with other more productive ways to engage in conflict. This exercise will help you both learn a little more about each other's histories with conflict in order to understand where you're coming from, and plan where you would like to be when it comes to handling conflict.

1. Use the table on the following page to describe how conflict took place between people in your family. Use the blank spaces for other relationships you witnessed growing up.

2. Circle the relationships that you identify as the "most successful conflict resolvers" and those who are the "least successful conflict resolvers."

3. Talk through how you made your respective assessments.

4. Together, decide on the top three things you'd like to use or avoid from your past when resolving conflicts in the present.

	PARTNER A	**PARTNER B**
Example: Aunt and uncle	*Aunt did a lot of yelling and usually walked away, slamming doors, but uncle said nothing.*	*Aunt and uncle never yelled and talked through things calmly. I never felt any tension between them after disagreements.*
Parents		
Siblings		
Extended family		
Other:		
Other:		

OUR CONFLICT RULES:

1. ....

2. ....

3. ....

The Rules of Engagement during Conflict

For some couples, conflict happens very calmly, without raised voices or a lot of negative energy. For others, it gets loud and energetic. Setting conflict guidelines in advance can ensure that both parties feel safe and heard and can result in healthier, more effective communication, even in conflict. This exercise tasks you with setting ground rules for making your conflicts more compassionate and productive.

1. Look back to your previous relationships and the relationships you saw when you were growing up. Your history (see Perspective Sharing on Conflict, page 94) can help you understand your current comfort level with conflict.

2. Together, make a list of ground rules for conflict engagement that takes into consideration the comfort of both parties. Maybe you want to ban yelling or not allow name-calling or blaming. Base this on *your* own experiences and needs.

3. Commit to adhering to these rules in future conflicts and to holding each other accountable.

OUR GROUND RULES:

Commitment to Healthy Resolutions

Conflict within your relationship is inevitable. You are two different people with different backgrounds, voices, opinions, thoughts, and interests, and that's what makes the relationship interesting. You will not always see things through the same lens. A healthy approach to conflict is when you give one another grace as you work toward resolution. The pledge below can help you commit to a more empathic, healthier approach to conflict.

1. Choose to do an activity together that makes you both calm (yoga, mindful walk in the park, dinner at a jazz club, etc.).

2. After you have completed this activity, discuss the ground rules you set in the last exercise (see page 96) for addressing conflict.

3. Customize the pledge as needed to include what you've come up with together.

4. Make this pledge to one another, and revisit it as often as you need for a reminder of your commitment.

A PLEDGE FOR HEALTHY CONFLICT

I pledge to respect our guidelines for healthy conflict, including, but not limited to:

In case I make a mistake, please remind me of these guidelines, and I will do better.

CHAPTER 8

Foster an Equal Partnership

An equal partnership means that both partners put in equal effort and appreciate each other for that effort. It means that each partner values the other's life, work, and interests. Defining and measuring reciprocity and mutual effort will differ for each couple, depending on their individual and shared values. This chapter offers a better understanding of what it means to have a balanced relationship. It will guide you on how to maintain that equilibrium through the hills and valleys of life. You'll define equity together, based on what works best for both of you and not what looks good on paper or what meets external expectations.

What Does Equal Partnership Look Like?

There is no perfect equation for equality in your relationship. Equality tends to exist when each partner has their interests and needs met. More specifically, equality looks like equal effort, support, appreciation, respect, and shared goals. Both partners feel satisfaction from the level of commitment in the relationship. Equality in the relationship also means that partners are on the same page and have taken time to align on their relationship goals and how they will get there.

Have you taken the time to check in with your partner regarding the way they perceive equality in the relationship and the way they would like it to be? There's no better time than the present. Answer these questions together:

What are our relationship goals?

Are we providing mutual support to each other? How?

Do we feel equally valued in this relationship?

Are there any areas in which we feel an imbalance in the relationship (values, support, etc.)?

Define Equal

The look and feeling of equality is very personal and unique to each individual and couple. Equality in a partnership reduces feelings of stress and anxiety and preserves relationship longevity. After all, having an equal partnership removes worries about an imbalance of respect and understanding and leaves both partners feeling safe.

Each partner should read through the statements on the chart, and place a check mark in the relevant column next to the descriptions that best define relationship equality for them. When you are finished, discuss your responses and other components of equality in the relationship, if any.

	PARTNER A	PARTNER B
I will do what I am good at in the relationship.		
Everything should be 50/50.		
There are times when one partner's needs should take priority.		
Each of our interests is respected.		
We should both want the same thing.		
What I want to achieve in my life depends on what my partner wants to achieve.		
We take equal responsibility for our shared finances.		

Our Vision

Your vision for your relationship focuses on your future goals. It describes what you want your partnership to become. For some, a shared vision may be to be best friends, giving other relationships a lower priority. For others, a shared vision may be to work hard and play hard, valuing quality time together on regularly scheduled vacations. In order to move in the same direction, it is critical that you have a shared vision and that each partner takes equal ownership in the execution of the vision.

1. Take out a magazine or print images from an online source that depict the way you envision yourselves in the future.

2. Create a collage together in the box below.

3. When you are done, tell the story of your vision box and talk through each person's role in making your vision come to life.

Both of Your Wants and Needs Matter

Equality in a relationship means coming to decisions that respect and consider each person's wants and needs. In an equal partnership, both partners should be comfortable advocating for themselves in order to reach compromise and/or resolution. Here you'll have the opportunity to practice asking for what you'd like in the face of competing goals.

1. Agree on a topic to be discussed, something you either haven't touched on or that has come up but not been resolved.

2. Use the Venn diagram to document your separate needs and wants with respect to the issue at hand.

3. Take turns talking through your needs and wants and why they are important to you.

4. Make a plan to incorporate both of your needs and as many wants as possible.

5. If you find that meeting both of your needs simultaneously is not possible, go back to a deeper, more vulnerable discussion of those needs to identify elements that are more flexible in nature.

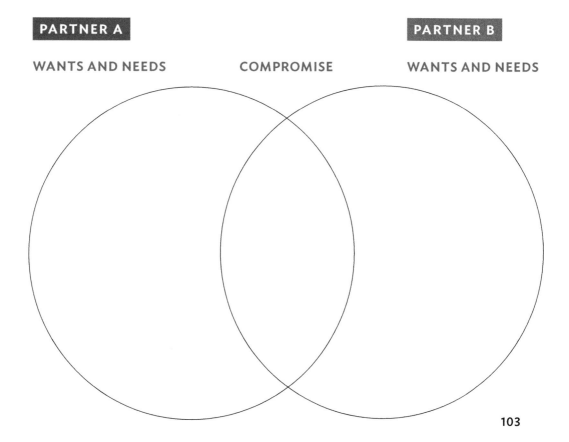

PARTNER A

PARTNER B

WANTS AND NEEDS   COMPROMISE   WANTS AND NEEDS

Equality of Care for Your Relationship

Healthy relationships require care, attention, and nurturing. As partners, you share equal responsibility for taking care of the relationship and ensuring your emotional connection. In this exercise, you will visually communicate what equality of care for your relationship looks like in order to make sure you are on the same path.

Separately, take ten minutes to think through the elements of your relationship and what's needed to bring it to full health. What do you each need to pour into the relationship? What impact will that have on the relationship? In the spaces provided, draw a picture of what your relationship will look like if you each care for it equally. Be creative. When you are finished, discuss your drawings with each other.

PARTNER A

PARTNER B

Why Equal?

An equal partnership in your relationship will help you avoid any uncomfortable imbalances between you and your partner. The resulting feelings of equity can result in less conflict, less dependency, and less resentment. Use this exercise to depict what equality looks and feels like to you.

Use the boxes to show your partner how you see the overall effect of equality in your partnership. Either draw or cut out and paste pictures from magazines or elsewhere that reflect that for you. Take time to discuss how to get to the "with equality" status.

PARTNER A

WITHOUT EQUALITY	WITH EQUALITY

PARTNER B

WITHOUT EQUALITY	WITH EQUALITY

Where Do You Need Me?

One aspect of equality in a partnership is having mutual respect and offering support for each other's interests, character, values, goals, and more. Without an equity of respect, resentments can form. This exercise lets you explore moments when you did not feel that support and allows you both a do-over, to support each other the way you needed.

To complete this exercise, take some time to think through one instance where you each felt the other did not demonstrate equal respect for you. Write down what the experience looked and felt like from your perspective. Finally, write down what you would have liked to have received from your partner in that instance and moving forward.

PARTNER A

The instance in which I did not feel equal respect:

When it happened, I thought:

What I needed from you was:

PARTNER B

The instance in which I did not feel equal respect:

When it happened, I thought:

What I needed from you was:

The Puzzle of Equal Partnership

Equal partnership can sometimes be puzzling. The term "equal" in a relationship can mean something different for different partners. Working on alignment on this topic requires transparent discussions. In this exercise, you and your partner will work together to decide on a concise way to describe how each word relates to the idea of equal partnership. This will build upon what you've learned in this chapter and challenge you to discuss further.

The answers to the crossword puzzle have been provided, but the clues are left open for you to solve. Work together to create clues for the answers provided.

ACROSS

1. ....

2. ....

3. ....

DOWN

1. ....

2. ....

3. ....

4. ....

5. ....

Separation of Responsibilities

Equity is an important element of a healthy relationship. Neither of you should feel like you carry an unequal load when it comes to shared experiences like living, planning, and logistics. The split does not have to be equal but must feel equitable. And the only true measurement of that equity is how it makes you both feel. In this exercise, you will look at responsibilities shared in your relationship and talk through an equitable distribution to avoid either partner feeling too much of a burden.

1. Talk about how your family of origin split everything from planning to managing the household. What role did each person play? Is there anything that worked well about the process or that you think could have been better? Share your memories around this subject.

2. List tasks that are important to the maintenance of your lives and relationship.

3. Use the Venn diagram to identify if each task belongs to one of you or if it is shared. Look at the completed diagram and discuss how responsibilities fall. Make sure neither of you feels devalued, overwhelmed, or taken for granted.

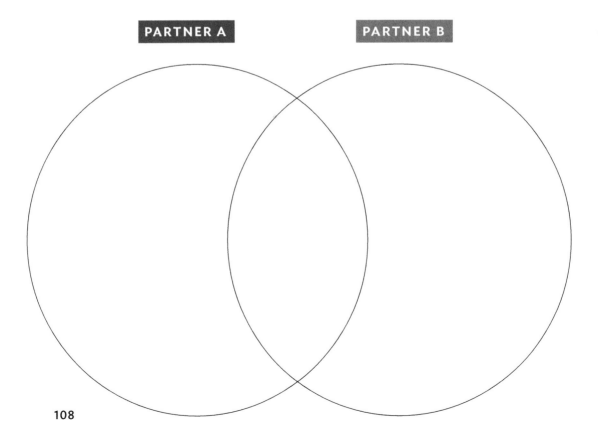

Balancing Self and Others

Interdependence, one aspect of equal partnership, is present when you and your partner rely on one another, and both of you are working toward meeting the emotional and physical needs of the other. To enhance interdependence, each of you must maintain your self-awareness, your relationships with others, and your boundaries, but still check in with your partner. This exercise services interdependence by planning and executing a joint "status of the individuals/relationship" conversation.

1. Agree to a time to get together with the sole purpose of communicating, no more than one hour to keep the meeting concise.

2. Before the meeting, make a list of items you'd like to discuss in the following categories:

   a. About me

   b. About us

   c. My needs

3. Share your items to create a combined agenda below.

4. Start the meeting expressing gratitude or acknowledging something positive about your relationship. When in discussion, practice effective communication strategies, avoiding criticism, defensiveness, and anything dismissive. Ensure that you leave the meeting feeling as though you have been heard, and you have been listening and responding equally.

OUR AGENDA:

Commitment to Equality

This pledge states that you will ensure equal partnership in your relationship. The specifics of this equality differ from relationship to relationship. But what does not differ is the emphasis on you as a team. And as with any other team, aligning your goals and tactics is critical. This statement initiates action to your commitment to equality in your relationship.

1. Choose to do any activity, but make the decision together, equally.

2. Before meeting for your chosen activity, reflect on what equality looks like in your relationship based on the exercises in this chapter. Read the pledge together and decide how to customize it to your relationship.

3. Take the pledge to each other.

EQUALITY PLEDGE

I pledge to trust and honor you as an equal partner. I will own my share of our partnership goals and communicate in a non-critical way when I feel any inequality. I will listen to your feedback when you tell me you feel imbalance. At times, I may have to carry a heavier part of the load, but I know there will be times that you will do the same. I appreciate your contribution to our lives together.

CHAPTER 9

Nurture Intimacy

Intimacy in a relationship includes sexual connection, but it also includes emotional and mental closeness. Emotional intimacy makes you both feel safe in your relationship through shared vulnerability and transparency. Mental intimacy means seeing and valuing things similarly. All forms of intimacy are vital to a healthy relationship because they create a unique bond between you and your partner, leading to greater trust, vulnerability, and acceptance. Building and improving intimacy is an ongoing effort. Intimacy can be, well, *intimate* to talk about, which may cause some discomfort. The exercises in this chapter will guide you to explore this type of connection with minimal discomfort and will challenge you to connect openly on a deeper level.

Getting to Know You

Whether you're newly engaging in an intimate relationship or in the midst of one, it's important to take time to discuss each other's relevant histories and needs. This information should not be used to judge one another but rather to understand what kind of intimacy you each appreciate and how you prefer to receive love in intimate ways.

Individually, on a separate piece of paper, answer these questions as you think your partner would answer them. When finished, go through each question together. For each incorrect answer, write what you learned today about your partner in the space provided.

1. What made you fall in love with your partner?

2. What is the first thing you noticed about your partner?

3. How do you show love?

4. How do you like to be shown love?

5. What is your favorite body part of your partner?

6. What is your favorite sexual memory with your partner?

7. What is your favorite place to be touched intimately?

8. When was your first sexual experience?

9. How does intimacy make you feel?

10. What is the closest you've ever felt to your partner?

11. How much of your intimacy do you want to be sexual versus emotional?

Commitment to Daily Intimacy Tracker

The measure of intimacy in your relationship is the closeness that you feel to each other. It builds over time through large and small intimate moments and gestures and includes both physical and emotional components. In your relationship, you and your partner may see intimacy differently. That is why it is so critical to talk about it, your needs, and expectations. Use this exercise to focus on your intimate connections and talk about your personal experiences this week to improve your intimacy.

1. Use the tracker below to document for a week intimate gestures you received from your partner and intimate moments you shared. You are each provided a column and your experiences do not need to match.

2. At the end of the week, talk through your perspectives on the experiences you documented and what they meant to you.

	PARTNER A	PARTNER B
Day 1		
Day 2		
Day 3		
Day 4		
Day 5		
Day 6		
Day 7		

Our Recipe for Intimacy

Intimacy is a bit like a recipe; it can be fine-tuned. So, it's important to talk through your expectations for intimacy early and continually as the relationship evolves. After all, what you want can change over time. Desires that might have been skewed more toward physical intimacy at one time might be skewed more toward emotional intimacy at another time. It is up to you both to determine what works best in your partnership now.

1. Discuss the physical, emotional, and mental components of intimacy that you each currently find most rewarding. These should be the bulk of your recipe.

2. Acknowledge any areas of intimacy you find less rewarding in your relationship. These should have less of a place in the recipe.

3. Together, complete the recipe card. Capture what you both agree you need most right now within the bounds of your individual comfort levels. Be specific and have some fun with it.

OUR RECIPE

1 cup ....

1 cup ....

1 tablespoon ....

1 teaspoon ....

½ teaspoon of ....

A bunch of ....

A pinch of ....

In a large bowl, mix the ingredients until well blended. Place in a tray and bake until the point of satisfaction for both partners.

Emotional Intimacy: What Could It Be?

Emotional intimacy, like physical intimacy, is unique to each relationship and to each individual. And as with physical intimacy, it's important to respect boundaries. Emotional intimacy in your relationship optimizes your closeness and feelings of safety with each other for a stronger connection. This safe place, free of judgment or criticism, fosters trust. This exercise challenges you to identify how emotional intimacy is present in your relationship now, and then create a clear picture of how you would like it to be. It will help you build or restore emotional intimacy going forward.

In the left-hand column of the table below, make a list of the challenges you face around emotional intimacy in your relationshp. Then, make a list of ways you would like emotional intimacy to play a different role in your relationship in the opposite column. Talk through the ways to get from the list on the left to the list on the right, and take notes below on what you will put in place to change the way intimacy feels in your relationship.

THE CHALLENGES WE FACE AROUND INTIMACY	WHAT INTIMACY IDEALLY LOOKS LIKE IN OUR RELATIONSHIP

STEPS WE CAN TAKE TO IMPROVE INTIMACY BETWEEN US:

Share Your Love with the One You Love

Sharing experiences promotes a more intimate relationship. This exercise gets you up and moving together, with space to reflect on your experience.

1. Partner A should organize an activity to do together that Partner B loves. It does not have to cost anything or be out of the ordinary.

2. As soon as they return from the activity, Partner A should document their experience using the questions below.

3. Switch roles and repeat.

PARTNER A

Description of the experience I organized:

What I observed about my partner during the experience:

The experience helped me feel more connected to my partner because:

PARTNER B

Description of the experience I organized:

What I observed about my partner during the experience:

The experience helped me feel more connected to my partner because:

What Intimacy Looks Like

It is healthy in a relationship to try and be intentional in engaging your partner in intimacy every day, whether it be a small physical gesture of intimacy or a more involved demonstration of emotional closeness. The weeklong calendar gives you suggestions for daily ideas, but feel free to customize it for yourself. Commit to all seven days and see how you feel after the week is up.

1. Follow the suggestions in the calendar for the next seven days. Take turns initiating.

2. Have one partner put a heart around the days that felt most intimate and the other partner circle those days that felt most intimate for them.

3. Together, put an X through the days that did not feel helpful in your quest to improve intimacy.

4. Get creative on Thursday.

SUN	Share your hopes and dreams with your partner.
MON	Creatively say goodbye before leaving to start your day.
TUE	Give your partner a compliment.
WED	Send your partner a flirty text message.
THU	You decide.
FRI	Tell your partner what you love most about them.
SAT	Dance to your favorite songs.

Learning the Way You Receive Love

Love comes in many shapes and forms, ranging from words of affirmation to receiving/giving gifts. As partners, you share responsibility for figuring out how you each prefer to receive love. This exercise will give you space to think through and identify the expressions of love that speak most strongly to you both.

1. Using the list below, each partner can place an "X" in the boxes next to the things they identify as their own "needs" from their relationship and partner.

2. Next, each partner can place an "X" in the boxes next to the things they "want," elements that they would like to have but on which they are willing to compromise.

3. Discuss and determine how to implement some of these needs and wants with each other, and add your own custom item in the space provided at the bottom of the table.

EXPRESSIONS OF LOVE	PARTNER A		PARTNER B	
	NEEDS	WANTS	NEEDS	WANTS
Gifts on special occasions				
Words of affirmation and compliments				
Physical affection (holding hands, etc.)				
Spending quality downtime together				
Helping out around the home				
Other:				

A Compliment Goes a Long Way

Compliments enhance intimacy by improving the mood of the compliment-giver and improving the self-esteem of the compliment-receiver. Feeling good about yourselves individually enables you to see that you deserve love and are comfortable receiving it from your partner in the form of intimacy. Compliments show appreciation and communicate love, especially when they are specific and expressed from your heart and your perspective (e.g., "I love how ambitious you are; it inspires me to think big for my own life, too."). Use this exercise to practice your compliment giving.

1. In the space provided, write four different compliments that apply to your partner. (These can be emotional, social, psychological, physical, or otherwise.)

2. When complete, practice expressing the compliments you identified to your partner. Take turns.

3. After all compliments have been delivered, tell each other how the exercise made you feel. Did you hear anything you did not realize your partner recognized or appreciated?

PARTNER A

Compliments for my partner:

1.
2.
3.
4.

PARTNER B

Compliments for my partner:

1.
2.
3.
4.

Sexual Intimacy Tracker

Healthy physical intimacy has so many benefits for a relationship. It gives partners opportunities to demonstrate respect for each other's bodies, wants, and needs. It releases endorphins and oxytocin ("feel good" hormones) in your bodies. Sexual intimacy helps maintain connection, commitment, and affection. And the vulnerability necessary to take part in this type of intimacy can increase the confidence and trust you have in your relationship. The amount of sex you have with your partner, however, should be dependent on an alignment of needs. Be intentional to ensure a consistent connection, which leads to a healthier relationship.

1. You have been provided with a seven-day calendar.

2. Decide the ideal frequency for sexual intimacy that is realistic for both of you together.

3. Now, set frequency expectations for other physical expressions of intimacy (holding each other, sitting next to each other, holding hands, etc.).

4. For each day that each partner experiences sexual intimacy, mark it on the calendar.

5. At the end of the week, discuss what increased your connection and which days did not meet your objectives. Agree to talk about it and adjust going forward.

SUN	
MON	
TUE	
WED	
THU	
FRI	
SAT	

Words of Love

Words of love build intimacy by communicating passion, respect, and appreciation. They encourage a positive mindset in the relationship and reduce negative feelings or thoughts between both partners. But using words of love can feel uncomfortable for some people. In this exercise, try to step outside your comfort zone, embracing the creative and dramatic, to ensure that your partner feels love through your words.

1. Come to this exercise with a pad of paper and pen for each of you.

2. Take twenty minutes or less to write a short poem (ten lines or fewer) to your partner on one of the following themes:

   - True love

   - Compliments

   - Physical love

   - Custom (love theme of your choice)

3. Read your poem to your partner while making eye contact. Hold hands if possible. Take turns.

4. Write down how you were feeling when your partner read their poem to you.

5. Finally, take time to share how the words of love made you feel.

PARTNER A

How your expression of love made me feel:

PARTNER B

How your expression of love made me feel:

Commitment to Intimacy

This is an opportunity to make intimacy in your relationship a top priority. It is key that you do it with intentionality, considering each other's boundaries. This pledge can help guide your actions in this commitment to intimacy.

1. Plan a nice night out, whatever feels special to both of you.

2. Review the pledge and customize it together to make it feel complete.

3. Make the pledge to each other. Then enjoy your evening in celebration.

4. Revisit this pledge as often as you'd like, as a reminder of your commitment.

INTIMACY PLEDGE

I pledge to focus my time and attention on our intimacy. I commit to focus on you consistently and to strive to make you feel safe and desired. This will include:

A Final Note

Look at you two! You made it through this book, collecting and engaging with tools and resources to grow your relationship. Take a minute to congratulate yourselves for doing the work and doing it well, together. When you met, there was something that drew you to one another. But it took a dash of hope, trust, and commitment to decide to make that connection a relationship. Holding on to those qualities can make many things possible going forward.

You've learned by practice that vulnerability, transparency, and compromise will enhance your connection. And it is hard work that brings out the best in your relationship. Difficulties and conflict will come, but it is the art of resolution that sends the message to your partner that you're in this for the long haul and that there is safety in your connection.

Relationships take ongoing effort, and you've already demonstrated to yourselves and each other that you're willing to keep showing up and trying. Continue your efforts in whatever ways work for your healthy relationship. And don't be afraid to revisit this workbook for a refresher and reminder of this work and its worth.

Resources

- *The 5 Love Languages: The Secret to Love That Lasts* by Gary Chapman and Jocelyn Green is an incredible resource. It can help you focus on the love languages of your partner so you can love them in the way that they can best receive it.

- *Couples Therapy Activity Book: 65 Creative Activities to Improve Communication and Strengthen Your Relationship* by Melissa Fulgieri is an engaging book of off-the-page activities to help couples strengthen essential aspects of their relationship.

- *Eight Dates: Essential Conversations for a Lifetime of Love* by John Gottman, PhD, and Julie Schwartz Gottman, PhD, is a relationship strengthening resource to secure consistency in date nights and encourage more meaningful conversations.

- *Eight-Week Couples Therapy Workbook: Essential Strategies to Connect, Improve Communication, and Strengthen Your Relationship* by Jill Squyres Groubert, PhD, offers tools and techniques to improve communication and reduce tension in your relationship.

- The Lovewick app is downloadable for free and is an excellent, accessible way to encourage communication. It offers conversation starters, date and gesture suggestions, and more.

- *Set Boundaries, Find Peace: A Guide to Reclaiming Yourself* by Nedra Glover Tawwab takes a thorough look at a topic with which many of us struggle, namely setting and maintaining boundaries.

- *The Seven Principles for Making Marriage Work* by John M. Gottman, PhD, and Nan Silver, is an incredible research-based look at what makes marriages work; it highlights key relationship pitfalls and how to turn them around.

References

Chapman, Gary D., and Jocelyn Green. *The 5 Love Languages: The Secret to Love That Lasts.* Chicago: Northfield Publishing, 2017.

"Codependency." *Psychology Today*. Sussex Publishers. Accessed September 20, 2022. psychologytoday.com/us/basics/codependency.

Gottman, John M., and Nan Silver. *The Seven Principles for Making Marriage Work.* London: Cassell Illustrated, 2018.

"How to Build Emotional Intimacy with Your Partner—Starting Tonight." NBCNews.com. NBCUniversal News Group, February 5, 2020. nbcnews.com/better/lifestyle/how-build-emotional-intimacy-your-partner-starting-tonight-ncna1129846.

"The Psychology of Compliments: A Nice Word Goes a Long Way." *Psychology Today*. Sussex Publishers, September 14, 2021. psychologytoday.com/us/blog/evidence-based-living/202109/the-psychology-compliments-nice-word-goes-long-way.

Singh, Maanvi. "Some Early Childhood Experiences Shape Adult Life, but Which Ones?" NPR. December 19, 2014. npr.org/sections/health-shots/2014/12/19/371679655/some-early-childhood-experiences-shape-adult-life-but-which.

Tawwab, Nedra Glover. *Set Boundaries, Find Peace: A Guide to Reclaiming Yourself.* New York, NY: TarcherPerigee, an imprint of Penguin Random House LLC, 2021.

Index

R

Relationships
  goals self-assessment, 9
  healthy, 4–6, 13
  improving, 14–15
  nurturing, 10
  seeking professional help for, 17
  unhealthy, 7–8
  vision for, 102

Respect
  accountability and, 64
  areas of, 55
  of boundaries, 81
  communicating via music, 58
  defining, 54
  through encouraging passions, 60
  equity of, 106
  through getting to know each other, 62–63
  identifying disrespect, 59
  mutual, 5, 53
  pledge, 66
  showing, 56–57
  through supporting work life objectives, 61
  through understanding viewpoints, 65

S

Safe spaces, 16

Sexual boundaries, 75
Support systems, 79

T

Thought distortions, 34
Touch, 16
Triggers, trust-related, 28–29
Trust
  about, 5
  assessment, 22–23
  broken, 28–29
  building, 31–32
  commitment to, 35
  date planning exercise, 25
  fears related to, 30
  in the future, 33
  importance of, 21
  quote bank exercise, 24
  vulnerability and, 26–27

V

Viewpoints, understanding each other's, 65
Vulnerability, 26–27, 32, 40

W

Work life objectives, supporting, 61
Work spaces, 16

Acknowledgments

To my father, Hermann Duchatellier: You inspired me to always keep learning and showed me how to love by example.

To my mother, Marlene Duchatellier: Your unconditional love and support have made even the impossible possible.

To my husband, David: You have given me the space to explore my potential and pursue my dreams.

To my kids, Lauryn, Jillian, and Christopher: You inspire me to always be my best and to love deeply.

About the Author

 **Danielle Duchatellier Boucree, MSW, LCSW-C, MBA,** is a psychotherapist who works with couples to promote positive change. Trained in the Gottman Method, Boucree provides evidence-based couples therapy to her clients in her private practice, HOPE Psychotherapy. She is a featured speaker for The SonRise Project, which serves parents of children struggling with mental health. Boucree is also the founder of Hope Station (MyHopeStation.com), an online community infusing hope and positivity into the lives of women.